A Boy Growing Up Under The Nazi Boot And The Greek Civil War

By

George C. Kakridas

Table of Contents

Dedication

This book is dedicated to the two women in my life God blessed me with.

First, my mother, who raised and protected me throughout my childhood's dangerous journey, especially during the German occupation and the Greek civil war. My mother, Panagiota, the daughter of George Kaperonis, my grandfather, put her life in danger day and night to protect all her children in our family from the barbarian German occupiers who tortured us and killed hundreds in my village and thousands around Greece. She worked tirelessly to help me immigrate to America to live a life I never dreamed was possible.

Second, my beautiful wife, Katie, who came into my life in my new country, America. She is a woman with a heart full of love and compassion that gave me a new meaning of happiness I never dreamed was possible. This woman stood by my side in every facet of my new life, and together we built a family and a company through the ups and downs of life's blessings and struggles. Fifty-eight (58) years later, Katie is still by my side with the same love and compassion as the day we met.

MY MOTHER PANAGIOTA

Acknowledgments

Writing a book is not only an Author's hard work but the contribution of others who helped to bring his dream come true, publishing his hard work.

First and foremost, I would like to thank my wife, Katie, who encouraged me to write my story and inspire others to never give up striving for a better life. She was the first to edit my drafts before I sent them to my professional editors.

I would also like to thank Evanthia Papakyrikos Kartsagoulis for her enthusiastic help in publishing my newsletters and proofreading my manuscript.

I also would like to thank my editor and his team Alvin Alridge for editing and publishing my book.

WHY I WRITE...

I write because I woke up at 3 am one early morning to a nightmare. The church bells were ringing in rapid succession three times and continued for almost an hour until every man, woman, and child heard it. That was the signal that the Germans were coming. I jumped on my feet, ran to my desk, and started writing the story of my life, "Growing Up Under The Nazi Boot."

1. I write to tell my story so others can learn how difficult life is when you have no control over it; all you can do is try and stay alive.
2. I write to begin a dialog and converse with my friends and relatives who live far away from me.
3. I write to remember.
4. I write to forget.
5. I write because it gives me pleasure and hopes I did not have as a child.
6. I write because I promised my mother to always write to her.
7. I write because I can plan on a blank page like a child in a sandbox.
8. I write because, as a child, I wrote in a different language.
9. I write to remind people of the thousands of children in Ukraine growing up watching their families and neighbors lying dead on the streets as I did.
10. I write because I feel lucky the bullets whizzed by me and didn't take my face with them.

11. I write because I feel fortunate to be an American.

12. I write because it reminds me of my love for my wife and family.

13. I write because my words reveal how vulnerable and transient, we all are.

14. I write because I am whispering in the ear of the one I love.

About the Author

George Kakridas was born and raised in a small village named Vresthena near the historic city of Sparta, Greece. He grew up during the brutal German occupation, followed by the horrors of the Greek civil war.

Mr. Kakridas lived through the NAZI occupation and the Greek civil war and survived nine traumatic years of famine and fear of death. In 1956, he got the opportunity to immigrate to America. Once in the US, he worked hard to live the American Dream.

Mr. Kakridas followed his passion for studies and attended college. In 1968, he graduated from Northeastern University in Boston, Massachusetts, with a Bachelor of Science in Engineering.

After his service in the US Airforce, he became the founder and CEO of a high-tech company located in Lowell, Massachusetts; the company manufactured automation electronic equipment sold worldwide.

He is also a member of the American Legion Post 8 in Andover, MA and a Member of AHEPA (American Hellenic Educational Progressive Association) chapter 102 in Lowell, MA; its mission is to promote the ancient Hellenic ideals of education, philanthropy, civic responsibility, family and individual excellence through community service and volunteerism.

Today, he is a proud author of his first published book—his personal story of varying colors titled "Growing up Under the Nazi Boot." He is now working on his second edition book titled *A Boy Growing Up Under the Nazi Boot and the Greek Civil War* with new tragic stories.

In 1965, he married Katie. Together, they raised two children—Dean and Diane, while trying to run and grow a high-tech company.

In 2000, he retired with his wife in Cocoa Beach, Florida. Presently, both reside in Andover, Massachusetts.

In his spare time, he enjoys his hobbies which include writing, reading, golfing, fishing, and gardening.

Mr. Kakridas possesses great interpersonal skills and is always eager to interact with his readers. Thus, he created his own website (kakridasbooks.com). Also, he is very much active on his social media accounts and publishes a monthly Newsletter. He would love to hear his readers' suggestions and feedback on his published works. Please, get in touch with him through his email, website or social media:

Email: kakridasgeorge@gmail.com

www.kakridasbooks.com

Facebook

Instagram

LinkedIn

Pinterest

Prologue

A convoy of huge military trucks rumbled onto the unpaved village square. The long antennas mounted on the front side of trucks swung back and forth like wicked, willowy fingers reaching out to pluck us from the street. The trucks were lined up one after another as far as we could see, and the thick, black smoke and dust rose in the sky, blocking the sun and polluting our lungs.

My friend Taki said they must be Greek soldiers, but an elder woman who had her head covered with a black (*mantili*) scarf was crying and sobbing, probably because she knew who these murderers were. She said in Greek, "*Afti then ene elines, ene Germani.*" (They are not Greeks; they are Germans.) To our surprise, the elder woman knew more about the Germans coming than we did. We were too young to worry about anything more than the rules of the soccer game.

When the first truck came to a stop in front of us, the rear gates opened, and the Nazi soldiers jumped out with their machine guns pointing at us. Shouting in broken Greek, they said, "*Pou ene e pateresas?*" (Where are your fathers?)

Both of us said, "*Den xeroume.*" (We don't know.) After all, that's what our parents had taught us to always say.

One soldier raised his machine gun and fired a burst of warning shots in the air that made us jump with fear for our lives. He then shouted in broken Greek, "*Figete Tora e tha sas skotsoume.*" (Get out now, or we will kill you!).

Suddenly, we heard loud shouts, *Alt, Alt,* then a rapid machine gun fire. I turned around to see who they were shooting and saw one of my older friends Giani, falling face down on the hard ground. When I got there, I saw blood coming out from the back of his body and his head. A few women followed me, screaming and wailing because they knew no one could help him now. I helped to pick him up and carried him into a nearby house. This tragic and horrific event traumatized me forever, seeing my friend, who I was playing soccer with minutes ago, now lying dead on the ground, shot to death by the Nazis. Someone said he panicked and ran when the Nazis fired warning shots in the air. This tragic death of one of our friends was committed by the barbaric Nazi invaders on the first day of their invasion and occupation. It changed my life forever.

We just realized that this was the first day of many days and years of the life of hell on Earth. Millions, including myself, lived through the daily fear of death, hunger, famine, and sickness before the Nazi occupiers were defeated and left Greece four years later.

I still live the horrific memories to this day.

Map of Peloponisus

Chapter 1:
The Nazi Invasion

When I was a little boy, the one thing that gave me joy—other than my family—was soccer. Like other children in the villages of Greece, I played the sport with my friends every day in the Platia.

A Platia (Greek for *plaza*) is a town square and a gathering place for the people of the village or any traveler passing through. It is where meetings and events are held, and every morning the children gather there to play soccer. If newcomers arrive in a strange village, the first place they will go is to the Platia.

But the strangers that appeared that day were unlike any that had come before. Their arrival changed our lives forever.

My friends and I were playing in the Platia, enjoying the sun's warmth. I was five years old. We were all so engrossed in our game that we didn't notice the convoy of vehicles rolling into the village.

The Platia

It was only when the rumble of their engines had grown too loud to ignore that we realized there was something going on. We were frightened and confused; none of us had ever heard a noise like that before. When we turned toward the source of the sound, we froze and stood stock-still in the dust of the Platia.

Long rows of loaded military trucks were speeding in our direction, churning up a huge cloud of dust in their wake. The dust filled the formerly clear air, and the wind flung it in our faces, stinging our eyes. Those of us who breathed it in started coughing uncontrollably as though it were something toxic. We covered our faces against it, but it was no use.

I was scared, yes, but as children are, I was curious, too; I wanted to see how many trucks there were. I tried counting them, but as more and more kept pouring into the village, I was unable to keep count and could only stare at them in amazement. Who were these strangers?

On the front of each truck was a big antenna that swung and wagged with the movement of the air and the jouncing of the trucks. To me, they looked like long, evil fingers that were ready to yank us off the street.

Suddenly, as though from far away, I recognized the cries of my friends as they ran back to their homes. They were screaming and calling out to their parents, terrified of these unknown visitors. I looked around at the few other children who remained unmoved. Their eyes were wide, and tears flowed down their faces.

Then I felt something wet on my own cheek. I touched the place to check what it was. To my horror, my hands came back slightly damp. Was there water on my face? No, not water; tears. I realized I was crying just like my friends. When had I started crying? Why didn't I know I was weeping? I had no answer!

"They must be the Greek soldiers," Taki muttered, coming up beside me.

I turned toward him and saw that he was scared, too, but he was trying to be strong for the others. Before I could answer him, we heard a cry nearby.

An older woman appeared in the Platia. Her head was covered with a black *mantili*, scarf, and she was sobbing.

She cried in Greek, *"Afti then ene Elines ene Germani!"* "They are not Greeks. They are Germans!"

My friends, already scared, became even more anxious after hearing the woman's words. Taki and I looked at each other, surprised that the older woman knew more about the soldiers than we did. But how could we have known? We were all so young; we thought of nothing but soccer; what did we know about the Nazis?

The trucks came to a halt near us. The rear gates opened, and hundreds of German soldiers jumped off, running toward us with their machine guns pointing, shouting in broken Greek at us.

"Pou ene e pateresas?" they shouted. "Where are your fathers?" The Greek words sounded harsh in their mouths.

Taki and I mumbled, *"Den xeroume,"* exactly as our parents had taught us. "We don't know."

This made the Nazis angry, and one of them raised his machine gun and started firing into the air. We started shrieking; some of the other children were weeping.

The one who had shouted now screeched, *"Figete Tora e tha sas skotsoume!"* "Get out now, or we will kill you."

We needed no more urging. Our hearts were pounding in our chests, and we scattered from the Platia, each to their respective houses. Never had we run harder or more desperately than we did that day; we wanted to be away from those soldiers. We did not know exactly how, but we knew they brought death with them in those monstrous trucks.

Suddenly, we heard loud shouts, *Alt, Alt,* then a rapid machine gun fire. I turned around to see who they were shooting and saw one of my older friends Giani, falling face down on the hard ground. When I got there, I saw blood coming out from the back of his body and his head. A few women followed me, screaming and wailing because they knew no one could help him now. I helped to pick him up and carried him into a nearby house. This tragic and horrific event traumatized me forever, seeing my friend, who I was playing soccer with minutes ago, now lying dead on the ground, shot to death by the Nazis. Someone said he panicked and ran when the Nazis fired warning shots in the air.

What we could not foresee was that our lives would never be the same—that what had been in our Eden would become a sort of hell for the next four years. Whatever our sense of foreboding upon this first encounter with the Nazis, neither I nor anyone else in our village could predict the suffering we would endure during the Nazi Occupation, in which we experienced hunger, famine, and sickness while living with the constant thought of our approaching death. No one could look toward the future in those years, as there was no future to speak of. At any moment, one's life could be taken away. The Nazis' cruelties continued until they were defeated and had to leave Greece in 1944.

The other kids ran away, but Taki and I stopped halfway and hid behind a stone wall. We maneuvered ourselves into a position from which we could see the soldiers while remaining unseen.

A few minutes passed in silence. Then, suddenly, we heard dogs barking behind us.

Taki and I glanced at each other in confusion, our eyes wide. We were afraid to turn around, but we had to before the barking could alert the soldiers to our hiding place. Praying silently, I turned as if in slow motion.

There were two furious shepherd dogs standing on top of the wall. Their bare teeth and flashing eyes told us they were more than willing to tear us apart.

We cowered before the dogs and looked around for some means of escape. We were just about to make a run for it when we heard a woman's voice. She was calling the dogs, and the moment they heard her, they stopped growling.

"Come here!" the woman's voice repeated.

The dogs ducked their heads and, without a second look at us, jumped down from the wall and trotted off toward the woman's house.

Taki and I breathed a sigh of relief. The woman glanced at us and, smiling faintly, motioned us to come inside the house.

Taki and I didn't need to be told twice. We ran toward her immediately.

Only when we had drawn close did we recognize the woman. It was Maria, a close friend of our mother's. Her son, Niko, was older than us and also our friend. Taking a last look around in fear of the soldiers, she ushered us into the house.

"Go sit with Niko," she said. "I'll make supper for all of you."

We thanked her and ran to the living room, where we found Niko looking out the window.

Taki and I joined him. Their house had a perfect view of the Platia. We were able to see what every soldier was doing out there. The sight of them unloading their things made my throat tighten.

To the left of the Platia, we could see soldiers pushing cannons toward strategic defensive sites around the village. Those on the right were setting up tents on the Platia, next to our church. At the same time, the others were struggling to hang a large flag on the front of the church.

On it was a strange symbol none of us had ever seen. I would later learn it was called a *swastika*.

I was too young to understand what was going on. However, I was sure that things were about to change horribly. I felt goosebumps all over my body when I looked at the Nazis' expressionless faces. There was something chilling in those cold blood-hungry eyes that I couldn't comprehend, and it kept me on edge.

Glancing at my friends, I tried to see if they felt the same way I did. The empty look in Niko's eyes and the unshed tears in Taki's told me everything I needed to know. I was not the only one who knew that doom had arrived in our village!

Maria came into the living room.

"Are you both hungry?" she asked Taki and me.

"No, thank you."

We declined out of politeness; it was what our mothers had taught us. Maria sighed as if understanding that we were refusing so as not to burden her. She came toward us and kneeled. Looking at each of our faces in turn, she smiled in a motherly way.

"Come and have some avgolemo soup," she said. "I know you both are starving right now, so don't refuse the food,"

We couldn't refuse after that because she asked us so respectfully and also because avgolemono was everyone's favorite soup. It was usually prepared with eggs and plenty of lemons.

After Taki and I finished eating, we told Maria that we needed to go home because our mothers would be waiting for us anxiously.

"Thank you for sheltering us," I said.

"And for saving us from the dogs," Taki added.

Maria laughed.

"My dogs wouldn't dare bite you," she said. "They were just trying to scare you."

We were skeptical but didn't press the issue; we really did need to be getting home.

Taki and I ran up the narrow, winding road to our house. We parted ways just as we reached the gate of our home. My mother shrieked with joy as soon she laid eyes on me.

"Where have you been?" she cried, but I could tell she wasn't angry. In fact, she was scared; I could feel her trembling as she held me, and she wouldn't let me go; she just kept hugging me for far longer than usual. "I was so worried about you. I've been waiting for ages. I asked the neighbors and Themis's mother, but no one had heard anything from you."

I, too, didn't want to move from her warmth. I felt safe in her arms; it was a safe haven.

Leaning back, I told her what Taki and I had witnessed that day from the beginning, when the German trucks, packed with soldiers, arrived in the Platia to Maria's hospitality. My mother listened to my story in silence, her face shifting from horror to sadness and tears flowing steadily from her eyes. It was a nightmare for me, not only because I had to recall everything again but also to see such broken expressions on my mother's face.

***

The next day, the German commander ordered all the villagers to come to the square for an important announcement. Attendance was mandatory, so we all hurried from our homes so we could be on time.

My mother took my sister and me with her. She held me in her arms and clutched both of my sister's hands. My eyes scanned the faces gathered in the Platia. Everywhere I looked, I saw heartbreak and defeat.

All of us were terrified of what was to come.

Only women and children were in the Platia; the men had fled into the mountains. The commander glared at us, his eyes flashing daggers. When he saw us flinch and shrink away from him, he was satisfied that we were sufficiently cowed. He smiled and began a speech.

"Your village is now under the government of the German Army," he announced. "We will remain here until our *Führer*, Adolf Hitler, orders us to leave. It is in your best interest that you cooperate with us in every way that lies in your power. Any refusal not to cooperate will be punished. And if any of you dares to kill a German soldier …" he paused to let the weight of it sink in, "… we will kill fifty of you. And that includes women and children!"

The hard life under the Nazis had begun. We had no choice but to live under their rules—there was nobody to protect and care for us. The men were hiding out in caves deep in the mountains. The women and children remained in the village, fearing for their lives, not knowing how long we could survive without food and medicine. The elders, our grandparents, remained with us to offer counsel and encourage us not to lose hope, but it was impossible to have hope at that time.

Over the following days, the Germans began going from one house to the other, searching for men in hiding. They wanted to be sure we couldn't fight back. They also ordered all the villagers to bring their weapons to the Platia for confiscation, with the warning that those who refused to comply would be shot dead.

**

One morning, I was having breakfast with my mother and sister in our kitchen when something unexpected happened. The morsels I was eating froze on the way to my mouth as we heard voices outside the house. We all became perfectly motionless. A moment later, we heard the heavy tread of boots moving up the steps to our *taratsa* terrace.

No one breathed. It was like the quiet moments before a storm. We prayed silently, fearing the worst.

Knock.! Knock.!

The knocks were so hard and loud in the silence that they sounded more like kicks than knocks The three of us jumped to our feet. We looked at each other in frantic silence, eyes wild with fear. The Nazis were at our door.

"Get behind me," our mother said. "Don't speak, and don't make any sudden moves. I will open the door."

We clung close to her as she moved toward the door handle. But then, just as she placed her hand on the knob, the door flew open into the house. The Nazi, finding his knock unanswered, had brutally kicked in the door.

A deafening *bang!* reverberated through the kitchen. The whole house shook; dishes and glasses fell off the kitchen table, scattering shards of glass all over the concrete floor. The door had come off its hinges, knocking our mother to the floor—and the door fell on top of her.

Niki and I hugged each other and trembled. Had they killed our mother? Would they kill us next?

There were two Nazi soldiers in our house; they seemed to fill the whole kitchen. They were glaring at us with venom, almost hatred, and though they were speaking to us, we could not make out what they were saying—it just sounded like animal growling to us, as though they were beasts rather than men.

Neither of them showed any regard for our mother, who might have been dying under the heavy door. My sister and I feared that she was already dead. Her body lay motionless; the door did not stir. We were anxious to go to her and see if she was all right, but we didn't dare move under the soldiers' glares.

The soldiers scanned our house, gauging everything. When they were finished, they both pointed their guns at us.

"Where are the men and guns?" they shouted angrily.

We didn't respond. They brought the muzzles of their guns closer to our faces. My sister and I were paralyzed; we could not speak for fear. Niki started shaking her head from left to right, and I copied her. We tried to tell them we didn't know anything.

Den xeroume, we were supposed to say. But we couldn't say it. Not with our mother lying there under the door.

That was what our elders and mothers had taught us as children. We were not supposed to tell the Nazis anything about our fathers and brothers.

The soldiers grunted and huffed angrily. They talked among themselves and began moving from room to room, searching. As soon as they disappeared from our sight, Niki and I ran toward our mother. Together, we lifted the heavy door from her body, only to recoil in horror. Our mother was lying on the floor, face up, with her eyes closed and blood running down her face onto the floor.

Niki and I stared at each other, each filled with the same fear: that our mother was dead.

Hurriedly, Niki tore pieces from my shirt and wrapped it around our mother's head to stop the bleeding. We waited patiently beside her, calling to her over and over. She didn't respond. We both started crying.

We were about to lose hope. Then a miracle happened.

Mother's eyelids fluttered. A few seconds later, she blinked her eyes open. Niki and I were still crying, but now they were tears of happiness and relief.

Mother gazed at us silently. Her lips were moving silently, but it took us a moment to realize that she was trying to tell us something. We kept our attention on her and encouraged her, but she couldn't speak.

Niki and I motioned her to lie down until we found a way to stop the bleeding and check for any other visible injuries. Mother nodded her head and placed her hands on the bloodstained shirt, trying to keep it in place.

"I have a headache," she said. Her voice was faint and weak.

"What if she has more injuries?" Niki whispered to me.

"What?"

"What if she's hurt…*inside*?"

I shot an uneasy glance at Mother, who was having trouble even lying down. I didn't know what to look for—what signs of internal injury could a five-year-old identify? All I had was my love.

In the meantime, the two Nazis kicked down the bedroom doors, though, at that point, they could just have opened them. Niki and I did our best to focus on our mother and ignore the Nazis. Nevertheless, every minute or two, there would be a deafening bang from somewhere in the house—the sound of them breaking something or just destroying our house—which would startle us. They were looking for men and guns, but finding neither, they were simply smashing up the house anyway.

Niki and I checked Mother for broken bones or other injuries. We couldn't find any injuries, helped her off the floor, took her to a bed in the family room, and made her lie down.

"Rest here until they go away," we whispered. We had no choice; we could hardly move her while the Nazis were ransacking the house.

Mother nodded in agreement, then winced in pain; the slightest movement intensified her headache.

After a little while, we noticed that there was still blood seeping through the makeshift bandage.

"Press it, Mother," we said. "You have to press it down to stop the blood."

We sat there beside her, praying she would be all right and that the Nazis wouldn't kill us. In the background, we could hear the Nazis shouting at each other as they turned the house upside down. We could hear furniture smashing and dishes shattering.

The violent stomping of the boots indicated to us that the soldiers were returning from their rampage. It felt like hours, though it must only have been a few minutes.

They were highly irritated, and their angry faces reminded me of the mad foxes that my father used to catch in his steel traps.

It was clear they hadn't found what they were looking for, and they were furious.

They approached us quickly as if they were about to kill us. Both kept their fingers firmly on the triggers of their guns and shouted, *"Tin ali fora tha sas scotosoume ean den mas pite pou ene I andres."*

Meaning, "Next time, we will kill you all dead if you don't tell us where the men are hiding."

Then they turned abruptly, left the house, and ran down the stairs. They strode out of the courtyard door; one of them was carrying a bag on his shoulder. It didn't occur to us that they had stolen something from us until it was too late.

My sister and I were troubled to see those bags because they hadn't come with any bags, just their machine guns. However, the most important thing was that we were safe. That was the only thing that mattered. Niki and I hugged each other tightly. We started thanking God that we had lived through our first confrontation with the Nazis.

But in the back of our minds, we knew it would not be our last meeting with them. They were not going to leave us alone. And the next time we met them, it was going to be worse!

"Stay here with Mother," Niki said. "I'm going to go make something for her."

She went into the kitchen, careful not to trip over the broken glass or the kitchen door on the floor. She wanted to make some tea for our mother.

I was young; I couldn't sit in one place for long. So, I walked through the rest of our house to see what was left behind. Walking from room to room, I tried to stop myself from crying. The soldiers had wrecked our house. Seeing what they had done to our house almost made my heart stop.

It looked like a tornado had ripped through the house.

I turned around and ran back to the kitchen, shouting, "Niki! Niki!"

I rushed into the kitchen and took her hand. I started dragging her away to come and see.

"What's wrong?" she cried, annoyed. "What is it? Stop pulling me!"

But when we reached what served as our parents' bedroom and our living room, she went quiet.

Our eyes roamed over the devastation the Nazis had brought, seeing our mother's *prika*, including her dining dishes, smashed to tiny pieces, which were scattered all over the floor.

Overwhelmed with sadness and distress, my sister went back to the kitchen to finish making tea for our mother. I walked over to our neighbor Stavroula and asked her if she could come over to help us clean up the mess. The neighbor was kind enough to help us out. After several hours of cleaning up all the broken debris, we discovered that many of my mother's valuable items were missing.

The damage was beyond repair, but at least our lives were spared.

We later learned that we were not alone in having gotten this treatment; other families in the village had been through the same. What surprised me most was that others were treated far worse than we were. Many people were shot dead for resisting and not cooperating with Nazi soldiers.

Chapter 2:
My Life Before the Nazi Invasion

Why would anybody leave this beautiful village—a place with an abundance of natural resources, from pristine spring water flowing from the depths of a mountain to orchards of flourishing fruit trees? Why would anyone wish to part with the olive groves or with the lush grazing that served as pasture for thriving herds of goats and flocks of sheep whose meat and milk kept us well-fed in summer and winter? Why move from a land so healthy that most of its people lived into their late nineties?

Unfortunately, that is what most young people and I did in the 1950s after nine years of suffering under the Nazi occupation and the Greek Civil War. Only the elderly stayed behind to live the rest of their lives in peace and tranquility.

I was a little kid growing up in a small Greek village named Vresthena, located north of the famous and historic city of Sparta, nestled on the side of a mountain among green trees and green grass. A beautiful Byzantine Orthodox church stands in the center of the village, visible from all the roads shown in the photo and, on clear days, from Mount Taygetos straight ahead.

I was my parents' third-born. Before me, my parents had my elder brother Argiri, who was four years older than me, and my sister, Niki, who was two years older than me. My parents were farmers; growing up, I saw them working hard to grow our food just like all the other villagers did.

My mother was one of the women who juggled working at the farm and looking after her children. She would carry us in a *naka*, a sort of sling, to where she worked at the farm. Once at the farm, she would hang the *naka* under the olive tree near the well as a makeshift hammock.

When I got older, my mother told me a terrifying story. One day, when I was dangling under the olive tree, my mother decided to check on me. She would always keep an eye on me whenever I was in the *naka*; it was part of the daily grind of farm work. But that day, she was glad she did it.

As she approached the olive tree, she noticed a snake slowly creeping up the branch on which she'd hung me. Instantly, she dashed, screaming, toward the tree, still clutching her shovel. She reached the tree just in time to kill the snake as it was slithering into the *naka*. Maternal instincts took over, and she brought the head of the shovel down hard on the head of the snake; it lay motionless. She was unsure if it was dead, so she chopped it up into little pieces with the shovel to make sure it posed no danger.

My mother learned her lesson; never again did she dare leave me unattended in the olive tree. Unfortunately, she also learned not to let me out of her sight for even a split second; that one incident taught her to be fiercely protective. She was convinced that something terrible would happen to me if I was not under her watchful eye.

***

We didn't have a garden near our house, and our main meals usually consisted of broiled *lahana*, vegetables, and potatoes that were grown in the *horafia* farms or our grandparents' garden. We would also frequently eat *trahana* and *hilopites* as our main meal. The *trahana* was made by smashing wheat into small pieces and adding fresh goat milk and flour to it; it made for a nutritious meal that made us feel full and satisfied.

Traditionally made from crushed wheat and fermented goat milk or sheep milk, *trahana* was easy to prepare compared to *hilopetes*, which were a bit harder to make. *Hilopetes* usually took the effort of a whole group. Women in the neighborhood would gather at one of their homes and prepare *hilopetes* while gossiping. The gathering was like a mini festival involving women rolling and cutting the dough as they happily chatted about their husbands and children.

Most mothers in the village didn't feed their babies baby food from a jar. Baby food was not available in that era. My mother cooked all our meals, but sometimes, when she had to work late on the farms and did not have time to cook for me, she would feed me the same food she was eating. After she had chewed her morsel well, she would take it out of her mouth and feed it to me.

When I first heard of this, I thought it was just a tall tale and didn't believe it really happened. Soon, though, I was proven wrong; I saw my baby brother Mitso being fed in the same manner.

My mother was the one who helped me walk; she would take me up and down the stairs of our house. By the time I was three, I could walk downstairs to an *avli* courtyard where I played barefoot, sometimes going into the mud after heavy rain. I would play with my *topi*—a ball made of old clothes rolled up into a spherical mass that would swiftly unravel during the play and would have to be re-wrapped so that play could continue.

When I got tired of playing with the *topi* ball, I would go over to the rabbits' cage. My father kept them fenced in with wire mesh so that they wouldn't run around and be eaten by foxes at night. I was told never to leave the door open as the rabbits would run out, and it would be hard to get them back in the cage. I remember walking over and opening the small door of the wire fence, making sure to close it after me to ensure the rabbits were inside and safe.

I played with those beautiful little rabbits; I loved their different shades of white, grey, and black. I was fascinated by how they looked. Their big, round eyes and long ears standing up filled me with awe. My father told me not to try picking them up as they could scratch me. He told me there was just one safe way to pick up rabbits—by the ears—but I was too scared to do that.

My meet-and-greet with the rabbits was a part of my daily routine. I went there whenever I wanted to play, and as a side-effect, I also got to learn a lot about rabbits. I learned that they came in various colors and coat types and that some were bigger than others. At first, I thought my father had built the rabbits' house for my siblings and me to play in, and it was not until later that I learned the truth about it.

It was a habit for me to always count the number of rabbits in the cage, and as I remember, we had nine. One day, when I went back to play with what I thought were my toys, I noticed, upon counting them, that one was missing. I counted them one more time and came up with eight again.

I started crying and calling for my mother. She came running out to see what had happened to me.

"What's wrong, *kamari mou* (my dearest)?" she asked me, scanning me from top to bottom to see if I was injured. "What happened? Did you fall? Are you hurt?"

"No, *Mitera*!" I told her, panting heavily.

"Then what is it?" she asked again, frowning.

"A rabbit is missing, *Mitera*!"

"What?"

"Yes, I counted on Sunday morning, and there were nine rabbits, but now there are only eight of them! Where did he go, Mitera? Who could have taken him? A fox, maybe?"

"On Sunday…?" My mother paused, thinking. "Oh!"

Her face lit up as if she had a clue about the missing rabbit. She gave me an odd look.

"*Kamari mou,* my dearest, we ate one rabbit on Sunday for dinner," she said.

"But…but didn't we eat meat for dinner?"

"Yes, we did," my mother said, smiling sympathetically. "We had rabbit meat for dinner."

This revelation came as a shock; I was upset to learn that the poor creatures were being raised only to become our food.

Sometime later, when they thought I was old enough to do so, my parents let me go and play outside the main door or *mandra*. At the time, I had recently made a new friend named Taki. He used to live down the hill and would always come over to my house to play, as my parents didn't allow me to go over to his. It was always fun being with him, especially when we played with the *topi* ball together. I would like to mention that Taki was the only one I could have fun with at that time, as my siblings were always busy with their chores and personal activities. Niki used to be with her friends, playing with them. Nonetheless, she was always consciously watching out for me, and if I didn't listen to her, she would tell my father.

On the other hand, my brother Argiri would say that he was too old for any games. He would tell me what to do and what not to do. He taught me how to be the man I wanted to be when I grew up. My brother has been my savior; he is the person I have always most admired. He would always care about me, and he was the first person I would run to for advice.

The *avli* courtyard at Taki's house was larger than ours, and it allowed us to play with the ball more freely. He told me that his father had brought a real *bala* ball for him and asked me if I could come over to his house to play. I was tempted to go to his house, but I was afraid to ask my parents. But my patience ran thin, so I asked my mother for her permission. Needless to say, she was not happy about it and refused to let me go to Taki's. I sulked for a few days, and, seeing my distress, she eventually talked to Taki's mother and decided that it would be safe for me to visit Taki's house. They both made plans for the day, going over everything beforehand to set my mother's mind at ease.

"My little boy is all grown up," my mother said in a wistful one. "All right; you can go over to Taki's house but remember to be careful."

She straightened my shirt, looking for any dirt or dust. "Walk slowly, and do not fall or hurt yourself, all right?"

"Yes, Mitera!" I exclaimed in excitement. "Thank you for letting me go!"

I was happy; it was the first time my mother had trusted me enough to let me walk by myself. I didn't realize it at that time, but that simple agreement was the beginning of my road to freedom. After that, I was able to walk around the neighborhood and streets by myself. I felt as if I had become independent and grown up.

The next morning, I went to Taki's house, full of excitement, and he greeted me with a big smile. His mother had prepared hot chocolate for both of us; we drank it, then went downstairs to the *avli*. We didn't know how long we played, but we had to pause when we heard Taki's mother calling for us to come upstairs for lunch.

We ran up the long steep wooden stairs and into the kitchen, where Taki's mother had lunch ready and set for us. It included fresh goat cheese with bread, along with a large glass of fresh goat milk. It was the most wholesome meal I had ever eaten; not only was it fresh, but it was also delicious.

I asked Taki where his mother got the fresh goat cheese and milk as I didn't see any goats around. He said his parents were goatherders. I was astonished to know how hardworking his parents were. Before I left to go back home, I thanked his mother for the feast.

When I came back home, I found my mother pacing back and forth in the hallway. As soon as she saw me, the frowns on her forehead began to disappear, and a look of relief and contentment replaced the worried expression on her face. She came running toward me and embraced me. At that time, I couldn't understand what was going on and why she was so anxious.

"I was so worried that something would happen to you!" she said.

I was too young to understand the source of her apprehension at the time; when I was older, I connected it to the incident of the *naka* and the snake.

After assuring her again and again that I was all right, I told Mom that I had fun playing with Taki. I told her about the hot chocolate his mother gave us to drink and about the scrumptious and filling lunch of goat cheese, bread, and milk. My mother was happy to see me joyful. She said she would thank Taki's mother for taking care of me. She now had the assurance that I was safe at Taki's house and never again restricted me from going to his place.

One day, I was playing a game called *kavales* with Taki and his friends at Taki's place. The game consisted of three or four kids holding a pole and leaning against it with their heads down. Meanwhile, a kid (runner) would run around the circle of kids and would try to jump on the back of a kid who could not defend himself from the runner. So, Taki and I were in the circle that day, and a kid was running around the circle. He decided to jump on Taki's back, and to prevent the kid from doing so, Taki struggled to escape his grasp. The next thing we knew was that Taki was screaming, and his screams got louder and louder as blood oozed out of his eye. He had accidentally jabbed his eye into the nail that was sticking out of the pole.

The commotion drew Taki's mother down the stairs, and when she saw her son holding his eye as blood flowed down his legs and onto the ground, she screamed. Swift as lightning, she ran to him and helped him up, got on a mule, and took him to the village doctor. Meanwhile, I was terrified; I ran home crying. When my mother saw me gasping from running, she asked, "What happened, Giorgo?" By the way, Giorgo was my pet name. I told her what had happened, and needless to say, my mother's apprehensions about me leaving the house were revived. Taki was lucky not to lose his eye, but the scar remained—just like our friendship, which thrived until his death.

This was our life in the small village where I grew up and forged friendships, the place where I made fond memories that I still hold close to my heart.

My mother was her father's favorite daughter; her sister Theodora was married and lived in a neighboring village, Vambakou, about 15 miles to the north. Aunt Theodora was a lovely woman; she liked my visits very much and wanted me to stay with her and her husband, Panagiotis, in their house in Vambakou for as long as I wanted. Some summers, I spent more than eight weeks with them, especially when I was too young to be useful to my father on the farm. I still harbor great memories of my time there.

My grandfather, my mother's father, George, built my mother a house and gave it to her as part of her dowry. It is the same house we were now living in. There was a Greek custom where a woman had to give her husband a dowry *prika*; it was an old tradition even then, but it was important to abide by it. I thought that rather than a house, it would have been far better for my grandfather to have given my mother, at minimum, a first-grade education, so she could read and write. But a good *prika* dowry was what my grandfather believed was necessary for a better future and happier life for his daughter. A baseless belief indeed!

Mother felt humiliated every time she had to ask someone to read and write for her. My sister would take dictation for her, and I remember her yelling with frustration because Niki would not write down exactly what my mother dictated. I promised her that when I learned how to read and write, I would write her letters using the exact words that came out of her mouth. Sure enough, when I was able to read and write, helping my mother read and write letters became my sole responsibility, which created an inseparable bond between my mother and me that existed throughout her lifetime.

My siblings did not have the patience to write and rewrite her letters, especially to her brother in America. He was the man that kept sending us money, trunks of clothes, shoes, and other household items, and she wanted to thank him as my father never did; my father just kept asking for more money.

At that age, I had not faced any hardships yet. I thought I was growing up in paradise—a place full of fruit trees, green grass, and birds singing as they hopped from tree to tree. As if I knew what life in paradise was like! I didn't, but I loved where I was growing up, being raised by poor but loving parents on lavish green earth with flowers, fig trees, and cherry trees alongside our vineyard.

Ours was a small but beautiful village of more than 1,000 inhabitants at the time, most making a living working their farms and raising animals for Sparta's slaughterhouses, in addition to consuming them themselves. Some people—like my grandfather, George Kaperonis—owned large herds of goats and sheep, which produced Greek feta and other dairy products—the dense, delicious Greek yogurt and famous goat milk—earning a living out of selling these products.

Our Orthodox Church was a key part of growing up; my mother would dress us up every Sunday morning to attend our beautiful Byzantine-designed church, built with marble from the quarry near our village.

Our house did not have electricity or running water. We had to walk down to the neighborhood water source, piped from Dexameni our main water storage next to St. George Church, about one kilometer each way, up and down a small rocky, winding road, to bring drinking and cooking water home for my mother.

I was fortunate to have two great friends in my neighborhood: Taki, who you already know, and Themis. We were all about the same age and were good friends. We always played together—usually soccer. Their mothers used to let them walk together over to my house to play as I was not allowed to walk alone too far outside. When I was waiting for my friends to come over and play soccer in my backyard, I found myself sitting on the bench in the back of my house. My father had built it so we could all sit out there during the warm summer evenings and enjoy some silent moments together, especially on full-moon nights.

The full moon would usually be bright enough to read a book or to see rabbits moving toward our grapevine during the season. My mother or my sister would throw a rock to drive them away from the vineyard and keep them from eating our delicious grapes. Our mother would join my sister and I when she was not working on the *argalio* weaving machine. She used to make household items for us, such as heavy winter coats and blankets to keep us warm during winter, rugs, and other similar items.

My mother's weaving machine, called *argalio*.

My mother would come out and sit with us and talk about our future. She was worried about a "severe storm" that was coming. We thought she was talking about a literal storm, but as we found out later, the storm in our future was not the weather but war. My mother could not read the previous day's newspaper brought from Sparta, but she had good ears to listen to what people were talking about, and the rumors were that war was heading our way. It worried her a lot, and she kept praying for us, for our safety.

We were too young to worry about war; we knew nothing about it and enjoyed the cool, sometimes moonlit evenings together, watching the bright flickering stars up in the clear sky. The stars mimicked a Christmas tree with millions of bright Christmas lights blinking, looking like they were dancing to the music of the heavens. My mother told us, "You can only enjoy it in a small and remote village like ours, away from artificial light." A smart and kind woman our mother was!

Before my friends came over to play, usually early in the morning and before the sun's rays made it unbearable to play a fast-running game of soccer, I waited on the bench in the back of our house. I would be seen with my glass of warm goat milk with a *cooloorakia* (a Greek cookie), enjoying the panoramic view, watching what seemed to be a dark line following the contour of the mountain peaks, suggesting a borderline, separating us from another world beyond the horizon.

One day, I was sitting there, dreaming of the day when I could be allowed to travel over that borderline and see who lived on the other side of those tall green mountains. Maybe I could meet a few new friends to play with. Anyhow, when Themis and Taki showed up, I stopped dreaming and listened to their stories. Sometimes, they were chased by a mean dog, or they saw a fox running away with a chicken dangling out of its mouth and looking back to see if anyone was chasing it. After that, and before we got down to business, we discussed the rules of our soccer game—things like who was going to play the goalkeeper, making sure we had a well-packed *topi* (though it was never round), etc. The ball had no bounce; it rolled down the dirt ground, and at times, it unraveled just as it was about to cross the goal line.

We would play for a couple of hours until the hot sunrays forced us to quit, or my mother would call us in because it was too hot for us to play in the sun. The soccer field was a small flat area in the back of my house, not far from our vineyard, surrounded by wildflowers and artichokes, my favorite dish that my mother used to cook for us. She always warned us not to let the ball go in the artichoke plants and destroy our next meal. After the game, my mother would bring us a snack on the bench, and we spent a few minutes arguing about a goal that should have been counted because the ball unraveled just before it crossed the line.

This one day, we were up to the usual grind when a sharp light bounced off a small dish on the bench and blazed across our faces, startling us. We looked around to see where it had come from. Then we spotted a big shiny plane up high in the blue sky; it appeared to be flying slowly and silently until we heard the roaring jet engines. The sharp, bright light was now blinding us, but we kept following the slow light, our eyes moving with the plane.

We followed this strange phenomenon with the young eyeballs of three village kids that had never seen such a strange but beautiful sight up in our clear blue sky. Now that bright light was getting dimmer and dimmer until it finally disappeared from our sight over the horizon and beyond the tall mountains.

My mother later told us it was the sun's rays being reflected off the shiny plane. We thought the plane was beaming down this sharp and blinding light; we were all standing on the ground gazing at this beautiful big bird with long wings flying high above. Now the only thing visible was something white that looked like smoke coming out of its tail. We didn't know what it was. Later, my mother told us it was called a vapor trail—another new lesson for us! We were still in a daze, looking at each other with our mouths open. My friends couldn't wait to go and tell their mothers about this wonderful sight.

We all believed this was a miracle; our parents had taught us to believe in miracles. We started walking back to my house, still a bit dizzy from watching the light straight up in the sky. Suddenly, I stepped on some small loose rocks and found myself falling backwards; my head landed on a sharp rock. Seconds before I passed out, I heard Themis frantically calling to my mother, *"O Giorgos epese,"* meaning "Giorgos fell."

The next thing I remember, I was staring at my mother's sad and tearful face, and she was saying, *"Tha ginis, Kala pedakimou"* ("You are going to be all right, my boy). *"Pos esthanese?"* (How are you feeling?)

"Mitera, my head is hurting me," I said, placing my hand on the back of my head, where the pain was coming from. I felt a thick bandage wrapped around my head and broke into tears, fearing I was dying. Mom leaned down and kissed me on the cheek, assuring me that I was going to be all right.

Later, mom told me what really happened. "You fell backward on your head after stepping on some small loose rocks. I heard Themis calling me and ran out of the house and found you lying on the ground unconscious with blood gushing out from the back of your head."

My mother quickly picked me up, tears rolling down her cheeks, fearing the worst might have happened to me. She then brought me to the house with blood still running all over the floor and placed me on my bed, face-down and still unconscious. She applied pressure on the open cut to stop the bleeding. Once the bleeding had stopped, she washed the cut with rubbing alcohol, the only first-aid antiseptic available to the villagers. Then she bandaged the wound with a wraparound piece of cloth that she ripped from her dress; there were no first-aid kits or emergency rooms to go to and properly care for such a cut, which needed many stitches.

About a year later, on a sunny morning when I was five years old, I was waiting for my friends to come over and find something to play—something other than soccer, because we argued a lot about the ball crossing or not crossing the imaginary goal line. Sometimes, we argued loudly, and my mother would hear us, stop her weaving, and come out to make us stop arguing. She always asked us to just play nice.

When I heard a knock on the door. I knew it was them, so I yelled, "Come in; the door is unlocked." They pushed the door open and wiped their shoes on the mat my mother had made on her *argalio* before entering the house. This time, both were wearing shoes. We all usually ran around barefoot, except when we were playing soccer, because then we had to ensure we did not break our toes kicking the *topi*.

After we set the game rules and decided on the goalkeeper, we played for about an hour; then, a friendly fight broke out about the ball. Once again, the *topi* had unraveled just before it crossed the goal line. We quickly fixed the ball and continued the game while dreaming of having a real ball that could bounce and travel far with a right foot kick like the ones used by our village soccer team. Themis and I used to watch them play, wishing to play in that team someday.

Themis was dribbling the ball down the hard ground, about to kick the ball into the imaginary net, with Taki tending the goal line. Right then, Themis's foot froze in the air because I yelled, "Look, look!"

A plane, flying low and fast, was headed straight at us. Themis'
foot fell to the ground and turned in the direction I was pointing; the
roaring engine forced us to plug our ears as the plane flew over our heads
toward the village.

We all stood there like three scared rabbits, ready to run for cover
but too frightened to run because the plane and its deafening engine roar
had immobilized us. It was unlike the large shiny plane high in the sky we
had seen a long time ago. This was the first time we had seen a plane so
big flying so low and so fast. Minutes later, we heard loud explosions
coming from the village, followed by billows of black smoke and red
flames shooting up toward the sky. We froze in our places, scared to death,
watching as our neighbors' houses caught fire and people fled their homes,
fearing their houses would be next.

Then another loud, urgent voice broke the horrific scene unfolding
in front of our young eyes. It was my mother, urgently calling us to run
back into the house and down to the basement (*katoi*) and hide behind the
stone wall.

"This time, it is not a flying mirror-in-the-sky plane like the one
you watched a year ago. This time, it is a warplane dropping bombs and
destroying our village."

Just before we ran back inside the house, I heard Themis scream
in a voice filled with terror, "Look, look! Another plane!"

I turned and saw a second plane flying low and very fast, coming
directly toward us. It passed right over our heads, so close that we could
see a red flag painted on its side and tail. Later, my mother told me we had
seen the Nazi swastika flag. As they were flying right overhead, I could
see the pilot as he dived and dropped bombs on houses not far away from

us. We could hear the loud explosions and the shrapnel whizzing by us. It was time for us to run down to our basement before we got killed.

A German Fighter Plane

After the plane was done dropping bombs, the pilot turned the plane around and came towards us in a thundering and defining sound with its machine guns firing and strafing the ground as villagers tried to escape the slaughter. Sadly, many were caught in the hail of bullets that ripped their bodies to small pieces. It was a harrowing sight for two five-year-old kids to watch and comprehend why this horrible thing was happening. We were too young to understand why humans started wars and slaughtered each other.

My mother now urged my sister and I to go down the *katoi* (basement) as we both were struck with the fear of death.

"Make sure you hide behind the stone wall and stay there until I come back," mother said.

"Where are you going, Mitera?" I said. "Stay with us."

I said so because fear had filled our hearts.

"I am going down the street to see if I can help any of the wounded villagers," my mother said. "They are mostly dead, but maybe someone is still alive and needs help."

She then quickly ran up the stairs while we crawled behind the stone wall to wait for our mother's return.

About an hour later, Mom returned, but that single hour seemed like an eternity to us. We spent it trembling with fear, dreading that something bad would happen to our mother and that we would be left alone for the Germans to slaughter.

Thankfully, Mom finally came walking down the stairs to the *katoi* with fear and hopelessness written all over her sad face and bloodstains all over her arms. She was holding a badly disfigured baby that she had found among the many disfigured dead bodies scattered all over the street, which looked like a flock of blackbirds shot down from the sky. Mother was trying to bring this baby back to life, but it was too late. She stood there helplessly, staring at the motionless baby in her arms.

That day, our lives changed forever; hunger, torture, and sickness took the lives of hundreds of my villagers and thousands of fellow Greeks for the next four years of the occupation.

THIS WAS THE BEGINNING OF THE NAZI INVASION OF GREECE IN APRIL OF 1941.

Chapter 3:
Life Under the Occupation

In 1941, the Nazis invaded and occupied Greece; soon after, the KKE (the Greek communist party) organized and led several groups of the Greek resistance. These resistance groups became a big problem to the occupation forces, Nazis, Italians, and Bulgarians by conducting daily ambushes, killing many occupying soldiers. thereby destroying and disrupting their operations. To discourage and prevent such attacks by the *andartes*, the Nazis retaliated harshly against the civilian populations by rounding up women and children in the squares and torturing and brutally executing them. The Nazis ordered that ten civilians would be executed for every Nazi soldier killed. Still, when they realized this measure was not working, they raised the retaliation killings to fifty villagers for every Nazi killed by the *andartes* or civilians. It didn't matter to them.

Regardless of the harsh retaliations, the resistance had become a significant problem for the Axis Powers—mainly the German troops— being confronted with one of World War II's most severe difficulties from the start of the occupation: "guerilla warfare." The issue of coping with the civilian population in seized territories was closely related to this. As a result, their primary purpose was to cut off domestic resistance before it could grow any larger and become an uncontrolled threat.

To deal with the guerilla problem, Hitler decided to install a domestic puppet state, the most cost-effective solution from the Germans' perspective. Therefore, General Georgios Tsolakoglou, who had agreed to a truce with the Wehrmacht, was proposed as prime minister by the Nazi puppet government in Athens. Tsolakoglou and his government of equally inexperienced generals had no prior political experience. Similar to the military ministers, the civilian ministers lacked political backgrounds. After the Italians seized control of a sizable portion of the country from the Germans in June 1941, the Greek people held the government in low regard, and it was plagued by internal conflict.

Gunther Altenburg and Pellegrino Ghigi, two Axis plenipotentiaries with the power to recommend the appointment and expulsion of Greek officials, were crucial civilian leaders in developing Axis strategy against Greece. The Italian 11th army, the German 12th army, "fortress Crete," and other divisions made up the military government, and there didn't seem to be a separation between the civil and military administrations. In December 1942, Konstantinos Logothetopoulos, a medical professor, took over as Tsolakologlou's successor. His primary qualification for the prime minister's office appeared to be his marriage to the niece of German Field Marshal Wilhelm List.

The first prominent Greek politician to work politically with the German occupiers was Ioannis Rallis. The Germans anticipated that Rallis would receive some backing from the pre-war Greek political elites and that he would be able to reestablish order in the nation and perhaps even work out a solution with the Greek resistance, ELAS, one of their major problems since their Greek invasion and occupation.

Ioannis Rallis created the Greek Collaborative Security Battalions in April 1943.

The Nazi occupation made our lives unworthy. Famine and hunger were our two most dreadful adversaries. People, most of all the elderly and ailing, died regularly. Only the young and able-bodied were hardy enough to survive—barely—and assist the sick and the dead.

My mother had run out of food to feed us; there was no grain with which to make us *trahana*, a nourishing cereal-like meal made from crushed wheat. She would send us out into the fields to find greens, and sometimes, we had to dig down to find small onion-like bulbs for her to cook us a meal. In the absence of medical treatment and essential medicines, many people died every day from incurable diseases like malaria, typhus, and many others.

Our daily lives were full of hunger and fear of being killed or tortured. When the Nazis came to our village, my father and brother would head for the mountain caves and stay there. They came and went during the occupation and typically stayed from a week to a month. My mother and I would visit my father and brother in the caves, usually at night, to bring them food and news from the village; they had no way of knowing what was happening around the country.

My grandparents lived with us, and the Germans often shelled the *andartes* up in the mountains at night. The shells that passed over our house sounded like thunderstorms. I was terrified. I would run to my grandmother's bedroom, crying, afraid the next shot would crash into our home and kill us all. The shelling went on intermittently, and I would wake up when another shot would go by and shake the house so badly that dishes would slide off the shelves and shatter with a sound like someone breaking down our door. Sometimes, I could not go back to sleep and tried to stay at my grandparents' feet.

The next day I woke up with the bright sun rays streaming through the window's cracked panes. I felt happy and thankful that I had woken up alive and thought that life was back to normal. However, a machine gun's rattling and loud sounds shattered the beautiful morning. It had taken me back to my regular happy place—the time when the only fear in my heart was if I could go out and play with my friends. Unfortunately, I realized I was dreaming, and we were still under the cruel Nazi occupation.

Chites was a notorious militia group of the extreme right set up in June 1941 during the Axis occupation of Greece.

The members of this notorious right-wing organization were Maniates. In other words, they came from Mani, a region south of Sparta whose people were known for their historic bravery in fighting the Ottomans, the Franks, and other invaders over the centuries.

Soon after the Nazis would leave the village, the *andartes* would come carrying their wounded and starving fighters. They would rest, eat our food, and use our medicine to heal their wounded. They took whatever they needed and left again for another war. Soon after they left, the *chites* would ride in with their trucks and jeeps looking for the *andartes,* and if they met someone and asked him if there were *andartes* in the village, no matter what his answer was, he was gunned down.

It was our new life pattern, dealing with three different groups of killers. We had to be careful of what to say and do to stay alive, and at times, it didn't matter what people said or did; they ended up dead anyway.

At least when the Nazis left the village, our fathers could return home and stay until we heard the church bells ring, telling us, "the Germans are coming, the Germans are coming." Their trucks would appear on our roads, heading our way. Our lives would, once again, be in the hands of the occupiers for as long as they planned to be with us.

KKE, the Greek communist party leadership, recognized the need for women to carry out many essential jobs, such as nursing, intelligence, and other vital abilities they could bring to the organization. They planned a full-scale battle to beat the weak and ill-trained Greek army. They created a new recruitment pool. They portrayed themselves as patriots working alongside the communist regimes of Bulgaria, Albania, and Yugoslavia to preserve Greece.

KKE targeted and recruited women, promising them a better life while serving a cause: to defeat and expel the Nazi occupiers from our country. It sounded excellent and patriotic to many women, but their plans were far from patriotic. KKE planned to eventually hand Greece over to communist Russia and join the communist bloc.

Women *"Andartes"*

At the same time, the *andartes* were recruiting new fighters when the Germans were not in the village and were targeting well-trained soldiers. The ones survived the fighting and defeated the Italian fascists, only to surrender to the mighty Nazis. Now, they had become an essential recruitment pool for the *andartes*. In many cases, they were successful because they were led to believe they would be fighting to liberate their country, but KKE was working on a different war plan, about which we later found out.

One of our neighbors, named Kostas, was one of those soldiers back from the Albanian border. He returned wounded and depressed about how the war with the Italians ended; they beat them and pushed them back to Albania, only to surrender to the Nazis' tremendous military power.

One early morning, Kostas was sitting in his kitchen, having coffee with his wife, and he saw two armed *andartes* coming up the steep stairs with their rifles on their backs; they just walked into the house without knocking and stood face to face with Kosta.

"Have a seat," said Kosta.

One of the *andartes* said, "We are here with an offer for you. We want you to join ELAS; it's part of the KKE. We want you to help fight to free Greece from the Nazis."

Kosta, having been in a war, fighting another Greek enemy, the Italians, knew the KKE very well. He knew that their master plan was not to fight to free Greece from the Nazis. Instead, they were fighting to eventually enslave Greece again, as the Ottomans had done for four centuries. Except that this time, communist Russians would be the ones enslaving Greece.

In no uncertain terms, Kostas said to the KKE emissaries, "I doubt you are representing Greece in this fight. Greece would never be a communist country. I'm afraid I will never join your false cause."

The KKE men then attempted to force Kostas to walk down to another house with them and meet their captain.

"I will not allow my husband to leave his house under any conditions," Kostas's wife broke in angrily. "Please, leave at once."

It was a bold, courageous stand for her; even though she was known to have sympathetic feelings for the *andartes*, she did not want her husband to join their organization. They left and never came back to her house again.

My friends Taki and Themis and my cousin Bill were bored to death with sitting in the house and playing marbles—the only game we had to play—as we were not allowed to venture too far from our home for fear of getting killed by either the Nazis or the *andartes*, not to mention Organization X, commonly known as the *chites* ("chi" is Greek for "X"). They were monarchists, and they joined with the Greek army to help defeat the communist *andartes*.

At least, that was what they led us to believe. Still, it didn't take a long acquaintance with the *chites*, who moved in and out of our village and always left many dead bodies in their wake. They traveled around Peloponnesus from town to town, killing anyone who looked like or was an *andarti* sympathizer. Thus, they joined the ranks of the killers we had to avoid in order to stay alive.

The *chites* were still another radical group for children to fear. At least this group was fighting the *andartes* that were kidnapping thousands of children, sending them to Albania to be indoctrinated into the communist system, and training them to hate and fight their own country with the Albanians. Consequently, our parents ensured we stayed home under their watchful eyes. The only thing we could do to pass the time was to play marbles; we could not run around the village because it would mean exposing ourselves to the *andartes*, the kidnappers.

Marbles were the only game our parents could afford to buy for us. We usually bought them with the few coins our grandparents gave us or when we earned them doing errands for our neighbors. Those errands were feeding the goats and chickens—if they went to a wedding or a funeral—or fetching water from a nearby water fountain and other similar tasks.

To change the boring game of marbles, Taki thought of another toy we could play with, but before we could play with it, we had to build it ourselves. It was Taki's idea to create a four-wheel cart, so we could ride it down a steep incline and have fun. His idea sounded fun, but who would build such a cart with wheels, and where would we find the wheels?

We had no money to buy wheels, so Taki's four-wheel cart was no more than an idea and a dream for now; it would become a reality only if we could build it without asking our parents for money and if they allowed us to play with carts outside our house. We all agreed we should wait until all our enemies, the Nazis, *andartes*, and the *chites*, had gone back to their homes to kill their people instead of us, and for now, we could safely play marbles in our house.

The Nazis were still around, so we only had to stay out of sight and fear the *andartes* and the *chites* when they were in the village. One early morning, when I was still in bed, I was awakened by a knock at the door. My family had instructed me not to open the door. My father went to see who was knocking, holding his revolver behind his back.

I heard my father asking, "*Pios Ene,* who is there?"

After a few seconds passed, I heard a rough, angry voice saying, "*Anixe barba Kosta, Eme O Kostas.* Open the door. It's me, Kostas."

My father realized it wasn't *andartes*, *chites*, or Nazis. He hid his pistol inside a cabinet drawer and opened the door.

Kostas was almost in tears, telling my father the *andartes* had broken into his house overnight. They had taken everything and left Kostas and his wife nothing to eat. Exhausted, he asked my father if he could spare one loaf of bread and cheese.

"*Karveli Psomi Ke Ligo Tiri* (a loaf of bread and cheese)," he said.

"*Pos den erthan Ke Se Emas* (I am surprised they didn't come to us)," my father said to him.

My father returned to the door with two loaves of bread and a large piece of feta. Kosta thanked him and apologized for coming over this early in the morning. He had to leave early to let his herd of goats out to graze.

It was a scary day in our lives, and I didn't know what my father would have done if it was *andartes*, *chites*, or Nazis at our front door, holding their loaded pistols. That time, we were lucky. After that, there would be many more knocks on our front door before these barbarians went back to their own lands.

Indeed, we often had to answer the door knocks. Every time God helped our family, many others survived this apocalyptic and indescribable day-to-day hapless living, but not all families were that lucky.

It was late 1944, and finally, we learned that the Nazis had been defeated. They withdrew from our village and our country, and the entire town celebrated the end of the brutal occupation by singing and dancing in the streets. We all ended up singing, dancing at the Platia Square, and drinking the homemade retsina wine. I remember my brother and me joining in the celebrations. However, our ordeal was not over—the civil war was still raging.

Chapter 4:
The Nazi Atrocities

The Monodendri Massacre - 118 Civilians Murdered

One of the most brutal massacres a few kilometers from our village was the "Monodendri 118." In that massacre, 118 civilians were murdered. It took place on the road to Athens near Tripoli, where the Nazis slaughtered 118 innocent civilians to retaliate for their soldiers' deaths in nearby towns. Several of those murdered were from our village.

I will never forget the horrific screams from parents of the dead, their cries revibrating throughout the village when mothers received their husbands' or children's disfigured bodies with missing body parts. The bodies were unrecognizable; they were blood-soaked and riddled with bullet holes, slaughtered by the Nazis.

I was unaware of what had happened. I asked my mother (*mitera*), "Why are those women screaming so loud?"

She said, "Because the Nazis massacred 118 civilians in Monodendri. Many of them were from our village. Their disfigured bodies have been brought back to the village to be buried."

This was close to us but only one of many massacres during the occupation.

The Kalavryta Massacre—693 Murdered Civilians

The Kalavryta Massacre was the most barbaric and inhuman atrocity by the Nazis in retaliation for the killings of Nazi soldiers by the *andartes* (Guerillas).

The Germans reached Kalavryta on December 9. In the early hours of the morning of December 13, 1943, they rounded up all town residents and ordered, "All of you separate yourselves as boys, men, women, and kids and get into the school building. All men move to the field." The field was owned by Thanasis Kappis, a schoolteacher just overlooking the town.

After looting the town and setting it ablaze, the Germans machine-gunned 438 men and older boys. There were only 13 male survivors because they hid under the bodies of the dead. Austrian soldiers were part of the contingent.

Then the German soldiers locked the rounded-up women and children in a primary school. After locking all the doors, they set the school on fire.

Fortunately, there was one Austrian-born German soldier. Witnessing the brutality of the Germans, he decided that he could not be a party to this madness. So, he disobeyed the orders and opened doors to the blazing school, knowing he would have to sacrifice his own life to let the women and children escape. Later, he was executed for "his act of treason."

The following day, the Nazi troops burned down Agia Lavra Monastery, a landmark of the Greek War of Independence.

A total of 693 civilians were killed during the reprisals of Operation Kalavryta. Twenty-eight communities, including towns, villages, monasteries, and settlements, were destroyed. In Kalavryta itself, about 1,000 houses were looted and burned, and the Germans seized more than 2,000 livestock.

The Kalavryta Memorial

Today, the place of sacrifice is kept as a memorial site, and the events are commemorated every December. On April 18, 2000, the then-president of the Federal Republic of Germany, Johannes Rau, visited Kalavryta and expressed shame and sorrow for the tragedy.

In 2021, a movie was released about the Kalavryta depicting the brutal massacre by the Nazis titled, *Echoes of the Past.*

Another Major Nazi Atrocity

In September 1943, German Wehrmacht troops slaughtered some 5,200 Italian soldiers on the Greek isle of Kefalonia. The massacre was a turning point in Greece and Italy's relationship, but the bloody event was downplayed for years.

The Burning of Our Village

Many German convoy ambushes were taking place almost daily, usually in the dark, on the narrow and winding road to our village. The Nazis warned our villagers that they would burn down our village if this continued.

Not long after the warning, the *andartes* again ambushed a German convoy near our village, killing many German soldiers and setting many trucks on fire.

The next day, they ordered all the villagers, "Vacate your houses immediately. We will burn your village to revenge for the deaths of our German soldiers because of the previous night's ambush."

A horrified and chaotic situation occurred as women and children ran screaming in the narrow streets, trying to flee and save their lives. Then there were others carrying anything they could on their backs, some just dragging anything worth saving away from the burning houses. It made for an unbelievably horrific scheme that still lives in my memory.

With tears flooding her face and trying to hide them from us, my mother said to us, "Take a few loaves of bread and anything else that you can carry from the shelf in the storage room. Run up on top of the hill and wait there for me."

My sister and I started crying, knowing the fate of our house, our birthplace, would no longer stand there minutes later. We put all the loaves of bread, a few heads of kefalotyri cheese in a sac, and a few other food items and carried this rather heavy sac up on the hill overlooking the entire village. We went up the hill where all of our neighbors were, including women and children.

After reaching the top of the hill, we saw our mother coming behind us carrying a heavy sack, so we ran down to help her out. She joined the rest of the women crying and sobbing while some held their young children in their arms. One elderly woman fainted before us, and others tried to revive her. Many had to sit or lie on the hard ground as they could no longer stand watching their houses burn.

We could see the red-hot flames rising through the roofs as they collapsed and burned to the ground. Black smoke filled the sky, and there was a strong stench of burning flesh, unbeknownst whether it was human or animals caught in the blaze. It was unbearable.

Some people said, "We should go to the next small village. We have no place to stay here."

We had no choice but to stand there and wait to see our home go up in flames trying to console our mother as she kept sobbing.

We saw the Nazis were now getting closer to our neighborhood and clearly could see them throwing lit flares through the windows and on top of the roofs. Within minutes, the entire house would be burned to the ground and turn into ashes.

My mother had heart problems, and she looked like she was about to faint. Worried, my sister and I asked her, "Mother, sit on the ground. It will pass."

We knew she had a history of fainting, and I remember my father had to give her a shot to revive her. To avoid another calamity, we helped her lie on the ground, and she rolled on her side motionless. That's when we realized she had fainted, but there was nothing we could do to revive her as our father was not here to give her the shot he always did. My sister stayed with mom while I looked for the water we had brought along.

By the time I got water, our mother had started to move. We helped her to a sitting position and gave her some water, which thankfully seemed to help her. We asked her, "Mother, keep sitting."

All the while, we kept a watch on our house. We watched women and children running from their burning homes carrying food and other household items they could carry on their backs, heading away from the burning village to save themselves.

Our mother eventually came around, struggling to get up. We helped her to get on her feet, which she did, but she still struggled to stand up straight. Nonetheless, we were happy she overcame her fainting spell.

She joined my sister and me in watching our still-standing house with tears flowing down our faces, waiting to see it burn into ashes on the ground like the rest of the houses. One by one, all the red roofs around disappeared, leaving nothing but ashes behind.

About an hour later, many around us were still sobbing as they watched their houses burn along with their hopes for the future. Our house was still standing, and we couldn't believe our eyes. After waiting for a while, we started walking slowly down the hill toward our house, holding on tight to each other, hoping and praying we were not dreaming.

We finally came near our house, looking for any signs of smoke or burning fire that may be simmering. Then I saw our mother doing her cross and praying to God that our house was spared. We all ran down the small path and entered the main steel door, up the stairs and into our house. We were full of happiness; happy tears soaked our cheeks, realizing our house was spared didn't know why, but it was not the time to speculate. We all hugged each other, not paying any attention to the stinging smoke flowing into our house from the blazing houses and the livestock not being able to run away. Our mother hugged us both and thanked God one more time.

We never found out why our house and a few others were spared. Maybe they ran out of flares or were satisfied that they at least burned down half of the village in retaliation. We will never know.

Among all these threats to our survival, my friends and I were still looking for a thing to do and take our minds off the daily suffering and killings by the Nazis, then the andartes, and now the Hites.

Chapter 5:

Hitler's Secret Weapon - Amphetamines

On the south bank of River Spree in Kreuzberg, Berlin, lives Norman Ohler, a German writer. He lives in an apartment on top of a 19th-century building. Norman calls his residence "Writing Tower," where he works and entertains visitors. The apartment—with glass walls demarcating it—is perched on the extreme end of the roof. Looking down through one of the walls, you'd see water flowing with Norman's boat moored far away.

The location of the apartment makes it possible to differentiate two sides of Berlin—one that is grey, almost showing signs of phantasm, and the other that is blustery and jabbing.

The left wall displays the Oberbaum Bridge buzzing with traffic; this place was once a cold war checkpoint. Further beyond it, there is the long part of the Berlin Wall, which is said to be the wall's longest remaining section. There is a large building opposite the bridge, which now houses Universal Music. A few years ago, this very place was GDR's egg storage facility.

Ohler sits at his desk, working; the light from his laptop illuminates his face.

Does all this press on Ohler as he sits at his desk, the light bouncing off the screen of his laptop?

Is it ghostly sometimes?

"Yes, it is strange," he said when asked about it, amused with the wooziness I felt and exhibited while looking down, standing right next to one of the walls.

Norman believes in time travel; he has had his belief placed in it for some time now. "I remember the 90s. The wall had just come down, and I was experimenting with party drugs like ecstasy and LSD. The techno scene had started up, and there were all these empty buildings in the east where the youth [from east and west] would meet for the first time. They were hardcore, some of those guys from the east – they didn't understand foreigners at all – and the ecstasy helped them to lose some of their hatred and suspicion. Sometimes, then, you could step into a room, and you could just see the past. Of course, it's not like that now. I don't take drugs anymore. But I can remember it, and maybe that was why I was able to write this book."

The book being discussed here is The Total Rush, *also known as* Blitzed, which reveals the bewildering and the almost untold story of the Third Reich's rapport with drugs, such as morphine, heroin, cocaine, and most prominently, crystal meth (methamphetamines). The book discloses the effect of these drugs on Hitler's final days, as well as on the successful invasion of France by Wehrmacht in 1940. Führer (Hitler's title that he used to refer to his position in the Nazi Party) was a total junkie.

By the time he recoiled to his last bunkers, he was already a hardcore addict with his veins ruined. The Führer, one of Norman's accounts, was published last year in Germany, becoming a bestseller. It has been translated into not one but eighteen languages – something that makes Norman Ohler euphoric with amazement.

"I guess drugs weren't a priority for the historians. A crazy guy like me had to come along," he said. Crazy or not, Norman has done an outstanding job. *Blitzed* is not only fascinating, but it is also persuasive. Probably the world's top authority on Nazi Germany and Hitler, the British Historian Ian Kershaw described the masterpiece as "a serious piece of scholarship."

His idea was to pen a novel, but with his initial visit to the archives, the plan changed entirely. There he found the documents of Hitler's personal physician, Dr. Theodor Morell, who was previously only a minor personality in most of Führer's studies. "I knew then that this was already better than fiction."

In the following months, Ohler traveled from one archive to another, carefully gathering his material, but he hardly got his hands on anything useful; nearly half of what he found was not used by him.

"Look at this," he said. He returned with a copy of a letter from Hitler's private secretary, Martin Bormann, where he suggested that the "medication" that Führer was getting from Morrell needed to be controlled owing to his deteriorating health.

The story told by Ohler is from the Weimar Republic days when the pharmaceutical industry in Germany was booming. Back then, Germany was a leading exporter of opiates (like morphine) and (cocaine).

Drugs were then obtainable from every corner of the street. This was when Hitler's inner circle began presenting him as an irrefutable figure enthusiastic about working for the betterment of his country, forbidding toxins from entering his body. He even forbade coffee, yes.

"He is all genius and body," an ally reported in 1930. "And he mortifies that body in a way that would shock people like us! He doesn't drink, he practically only eats vegetables, and he doesn't touch women."

It is no surprise that in a1933, 'seductive poisons' were outlawed almost instantly when the Nazis seized power. In the years oncoming, drug users were proclaimed "criminally insane." The state killed some of them by using a lethal injection, while the others were transferred to concentration camps. During this time, the use of drugs also began being associated with Jews. The office of racial purity of the Nazi Party asserted that the Jewish character was fundamentally drug dependent. Both these entities needed to be eliminated from Germany.

Nonetheless, some drugs had 'specific' uses, especially in a society determined to keep up with the spirited Hitler.

Dr. Fritz Hauschild, the head chemist at a company called Temmler in Berlin, was enthused by the efficacious use of the American amphetamine Benzedrine at the 1936 Olympics. He started to try and develop his own 'wonder drug,' and a year later, the first German methyl-amphetamine was patented by him. Pervitin quickly became a sensation; from train drivers to office secretaries and actors, everyone started using it as a confidence booster and performance enhancer, owing to the fact that it could be bought without a prescription in the early days of its introduction. Pervitin, as one would expect, also made its way into the confectionery. *"Hildebrand chocolates are always a delight,"* went the slogan. It was recommended for women to eat two to three to be able to get through their housework in literally no time. But that wasn't it; women also got the bonus of weight loss from it. Yes, Pervitin affected the appetite. Ohler described it as 'National Socialism' in a pill.

Needless to say, soldiers soon became dependent on it too. In his book *Blitzed*, Ohler replicated a letter from the year 1939 that was written by Heinrich Böll, the future Nobel laureate. He wrote the letter for his parents and sent it all the way from the frontline back home. In the letter, he begged for them to get him Pervitin, which, as he believed, was the only way he could fight his greatest enemy: sleep.

It was the job of the Institute for General and Defence Physiology's director in Berlin to protect the soldiers - the "animated machines" of Wehrmacht - from tiring out. After conducting a series of tests, the director concluded that Pervitin was the ultimate solution to the problem the exhausted soldiers faced. Not only did the drug rule out sleep, but it also dismissed hang-ups, making it easier for the soldiers to get through combats without being terrified.

A strategy was developed to conquer France through the Ardennes Mountains in 1940. A "stimulant decree" was delivered to army doctors, commending that soldiers take one tablet of Pervitin per day and two at night with a short gap between them. Around 35m tablets were ordered by the Wehrmacht for the army men and Luftwaffe, causing Temmler Factory to increase production.

Was Blitzkrieg the consequence of the Wehrmacht's dependence on crystal meth? How far was Norman Ohler ready to go with this?

Norman beamed. "Well, Mommsen always told me not to be mono-causal, but the invasion of France was made possible by no drugs. When Hitler heard about the plan to invade through Ardennes, he loved it [the allies were massed in northern Belgium]. But the high command said, "It's not possible. At night, we must rest, and they [the allies] will retreat, and we will be stuck in the mountains. However, then the stimulant decree was released, and that enabled them to stay awake for three days and three nights. Rommel [who then led one of the panzer divisions] and all those tank commanders were high, and without the tanks, they certainly wouldn't have won."

From this point on, the high command treated drugs as an effective armament by high command, one that could be used to bring the odds in favor. From 1944 to 1945, when it was very clear that winning against the cronies was nearly impossible, the German Navy produced a range of one-man U-boats. The plan was to send these tiny submarines up the Thames Inlet. Because they could only work if the lone marines routing them stayed up for days in one go, the head naval supreme command pharmacologist had no choice but to introduce a new super-drug. He began working on formulating a cocaine gum—the most solid drug German soldiers had ever consumed. This novel drug was tested at the Sachsenhausen concentration camp on a track that was used to experiment with new shoe soles for German factories. The prisoners there were essential to undergo 'walk till you drop.'

"It was crazy, horrifying," said Ohler. "Even Mommsen was shocked by this. He had never heard about it before." The young marines, Metal boxes strapped to them, the young marines were unable to move one bit. They were cut off from the outside world and experienced agonizing psychotic episodes as the drugs got hold of them. They lost their way frequently, which nullified the plan of keeping them awake for up to seven days because even if they were awake, they weren't in their senses or in control of themselves.

"It was unreal," Ohler described. "This wasn't reality. But if you're fighting an enemy bigger than yourself, you have no choice. You must, somehow, exceed your own strength. That's why terrorists use suicide bombers. It's an unfair weapon. If you're going to send a bomb into a crowd of civilians, of course, you're going to have success."

On the other side, Hitler was getting aware of his own incongruity with his only associate in the whole wide world, his curvaceous, unconfident personal physician, Dr. Morell. In the late 20s in Berlin, Morell established a flourishing private practice, having built his status on the modern vitamin shots that he loved injecting into his patients. After treating the official Reich photographer, Heinrich Hoffman, he met with Hitler; he sensed a prospect and quickly toadied himself with the Führer, who had been experiencing terrible intestinal pains for a long time. Morell advised Mutaflor, a bacteria-based formula, and when his patient began showing improvement, their inter-reliant relationship started. They were both isolated. Hitler, who came to be known as Dr. Morell's Patient A, only trusted his doctor; likewise, Morell depended fully on the Führer for his position.

Unfortunately, the same injection failed to help Hitler when he fell seriously ill in 1941, and this was when Dr. Morell decided to have an upgrade. First, Dr. Morell experimented with animal hormones injections for this infamous guy, and then he tried an array of even stronger medicines until, finally, he began giving him Eukodal, the 'wonder drug.' Eukodal was nothing but a designer form of opiate and a sister concern of heroin. Now known as oxycodone, its key characteristic was the potential to induce euphoria in the patient. Hitler began getting several shots of it every day, which was later coupled with two daily doses of the high-grade cocaine that Hitler was originally prescribed for his hearing issue that emerged after an explosion in the Wolf's Lair, his bunker on the eastern front.

Did Morell purposely make Hitler addicted, or was he unable to resist the addictive personality of the Führer?

"I don't think it was deliberate," said Norman Ohler. "But Hitler trusted him. When those around him tried to remove Morell in the fall of 1944, Hitler stood up for him – though by then, he knew that if he was to go, he [Hitler] would be finished. They got along very well. Morell loved to give injections, and Hitler liked to have them. He didn't like pills because of his weak stomach and he wanted a quick effect. He was time-pressed; he thought he was going to die young."

Upon being asked 'when did Hitler realize he was an addict,' Norman responded, "Quite late. Someone quotes him as saying to Morell, 'You've been giving me opiates all the time.' But mostly, they talked about it in oblique terms. Hitler didn't like to refer to the Eukodal. Maybe he was trying to block it off from his mind. And like any dealer, Morell was never going to say: yeah, you're addicted, and I have something to feed that for you."

"So, he talked in terms of health rather than addiction?" he was asked again.

"Yes, exactly," Norman said.

To the onlookers, the effects of the drug would look a little less than miraculous. In one instance, the Führer was so weak that he could barely stand up, and the next, he was yelling at Mussolini nonstop.

In Italy, *Blitzed* came with an extra chapter. "I found out that Mussolini—patient D for Il Duce—was another of Morell's patients. After the Germans installed him as the puppet leader of the Republic of Italy in 1943, they ordered him to be put under the eyes of the doctor." Norman once again sprang up, and once again, he returned with papers in his hand. "There's not enough material to say he was an addict. But he was being given the same drugs as Hitler. Every week there was a doctorly report." He moved his finger over the typewritten text, translating for me as he read. "He has improved, he is playing tennis again, the swelling of his liver is normal…it's like he's a racehorse."

For Hitler, however, a catastrophe was approaching. When the Pervitin and Eukodal plants were bombed by the allies, his favorite drugs' supplies began running out. By the time February 1945 arrived, Hitler was displaying withdrawal symptoms. His head bowed, he was dribbling and piercing at his skin using golden tweezers, and he did cut a sorry sight out.

"Everyone describes the bad health of Hitler in those final days [in the Führerbunker in Berlin]," said Norman. "But there's no clear explanation for it. It has been suggested that he was suffering from Parkinson's disease. To me, though, it's pretty clear that it was partly withdrawal." He grinned. "Yeah, it must have been pretty awful. He's losing a world war, and he's coming off drugs."

Two months after this, Hitler and Eva Braun, his new wife and one of Morell's patients, killed themselves, which is one incident that the entire world knows of.

"What happened to Morell? We know he survived, but did he get away unscathed?"

"I think a lot of Nazis did get away with it," said Norman Ohler. "But not him. He wasn't able to shed his skin, make a new career, or get rich on his memoirs, even though he could have said, truly, that he hadn't committed any war crimes. He lost his mind. He disintegrated. He's a tragic figure. He wasn't evil. He was only an opportunist."

After trying and failing to gather valuable info from Morell, the Americans dumped him in Munich in 1947. There, a half-Jewish Red Cross nurse picked him up, taking pity on his unkempt, barefooted figure. She transported him to a hospital in Tegernsee, where he passed a year later. Morell's maternal grandfather was a railway engineer during the war; he was the head of a small station in occupied Bohemia.

"One day at school, we watched a film about the liberation of a concentration camp, and it was so shocking to me. That same day, I asked him about the trains going to the camps. He told me that he saw one in the winter coming from the west and that he said to himself: these are Russian POWs. But since it came from the west, and he heard children, and it was a cattle train, he kind of realized something weird was happening.

"I wasn't much older than 10, and I was trying to understand: what kind of person is this, my grandfather? Because he continued being a railway engineer. He didn't join the resistance. He said the SS was guarding the train, and he was afraid, so he just went back into his little office to continue with his drawings. He always said Hitler wasn't so bad."

Norman paused. "You think it Nazism was orderly. But it was complete chaos. I suppose working on Blitzed has helped me understand that, at least. Meth kept people in the system without their having to think about it."

"It is quite a dangerous time. I hate these attacks on foreigners, but then our governments do it, too, in Iraq and places. Our democracies haven't done a very good job in this globalized world." That said, he doesn't believe the new party of the right (alternative for Germany) can pose a threat. "The right wing always had so little purchase here [after the war] because of our history," he said. "When I was young, you would never even see a German flag. The first time I did was in 1990 when Germany won the World Cup. So, perhaps this is just a correction."

Before I left for the airport, Norman agreed to take me to see the remnants of the Temmler Factory. We headed out on a bright blue day in search of the offcuts of Dr. Hauschild's white-tiled laboratory. We pulled up on a residential street about twenty minutes later. There were window boxes and net curtains everywhere, and it was as quiet as a graveyard. "Oh, my God," he said, stretching his long, slim legs out of the car. "Wow. It's completely gone," he said.

Ohler's research suggested that the Nazi leaders all preferred their own choice of drugs. When his book was published, Norman Ohler, during an interview with VICE in Germany, explained: "Not all of them took every drug. Some more, some less. Some of them were on methamphetamine—for example, Ernst Udet, the Chief of Aircraft Procurement and Supply. Others were on strong anesthetics, like Göring, whose nickname was actually 'Möring,' from morphine."

***

Norman Ohler, initially thought of writing a novel about the Nazis' infamous drug use. However, he had a change of mind when he went over the detailed records left by Dr. Theodor Morell, Hitler's personal physician. Ohler spent years studying Dr. Morell's accounts in the Federal Archive in Koblenz, the Institute for Contemporary History in Munich, and the National Archives in Washington, D.C. It was then that he decided to concentrate on fact instead of fiction.

These astonishing revelations about the Nazis being on drugs while they set our village ablaze and kicked down the doors of our houses while looking for men and guns brought to life many dreadful memories from the tragic Nazi occupation days. We did not have the slightest idea that these Nazis were under the effect of drugs when they inflicted torture on other humans. Now, I know why they showed no mercy or remorse when they machine-gunned innocent women and children in our village. Now I know why they behaved like wild beasts.

Chapter 6:

The Aftermath of the Nazi

Occupation

On August 20, 1944, the Red Army invaded Romania, and the German 6th Army was encircled and destroyed while the German 8th Army retreated into the Carpathian Mountains. Within days, most of Romania was occupied by the Soviet Union, including, most importantly, the Ploesti oil fields, which kept the German war machine running effectively. It was important for the Nazis to invade and occupy Greece in order to prevent the British bombers from destroying these oil fields.

On August 23, 1944, Adolf Hitler ordered Field Marshal Maximilian von Weichs, the commander of the German forces in the Balkans, that now that the Romanian oil fields had lost, there was no point in occupying Greece, and he should begin preparations for a withdrawal from Greece at once and on October 12, 1944, and by the end of the month, they had withdrawn from mainland Greece. Four days later, the first British troops arrived in Athens on October 14, 1944, under the command of General Scobie, and the Greek government-in-exile returned to the Greek capital. The conflict between the Royalists and the Communist Left soon erupted, which singled the beginning of the Greek civil war.

On December 1, 1944, the government announced that all guerrilla groups were to be disarmed. Soon after this, the Government of National Unity's six EAM National liberation front ministers resigned with the intent to register their protest, and in days, Prime Minister Papandreou himself resigned, and a new government was formed by Themistoklis Sofoulis.

This swift turn of events was the cause of the illegal EAM demonstration in Athens' Syntagma Square on Sunday, December 3, 1944, which turned violent when suddenly gunfire erupted, forcing General Scobie to order all ELAS, the Greek people's liberation army units, to immediately leave Athens, and on the following day, he declared martial law. The clashes ended on the night of January 5, and ELAS began a general withdrawal from the Greek capital.

EAM and the novel Greek Government conducted negotiations that ended on February 12, 1945, leading to the Treaty of Varkiza. This treaty provided a temporary break from open warfare, but Greece was in ruins, and the country remained politically divided and unstable. Some EAM members were enraged by these developments. One of the most prominent members who was infuriated was Velouchiotis; the Communist Party denounced him, causing him to continue his guerrilla activity. A few months down the road, the government units hunted and executed Velouchiotis. The policy for Axis collaborators was probably more lenient than the rest of Europe. The head of the special security police during the war and a Panglao follower, Alexandros Lambo, was given the death sentence, while most co-defendants of him received shorter sentences in prison. In 1945 alone, over 80,000 people were indicted.

The wartime collaborators were sentenced lightly by the judge, while the leftists were sentenced very harshly. The majority of these judges were those who had served during the occupation period. The appointment of Zervas as a minister was opposed by USA and UK intelligence because they were suspicious of Zervas' collaboration with Nazi Germany. It took Greece the longest to recover from the Axis occupation and the devastation caused by World War II as compared to the rest of Europe.

About ten percent of seven million people in Greece died during the occupation and conflicts. The hygiene and health situation were in total chaos, with sanitation conditions alarming. Those who survived the deplorable sanitation were also later affected by diseases like malaria and tuberculosis, falling prey to the lack of medicines, medical equipment, and medical facilities, malnourishment, and the total foundering of preventive measures. About seventy five percent of the villages had been burned, with more than ninety thousand buildings demolished or destroyed. Approximately seven hundred thousand of the total Greek population of seven million were refugees who did not have the necessities of life. In 1945, the country evaded famine very narrowly, thanks to the massive aid provided United Nations Relief and Rehabilitation Administration and the Allies.

As the battle lines congregated in Berlin in the last days of World War II, serious combat and vehemence erupted across liberated Europe. The blood-spattered events that occurred on Sunday, December 3, 1944, called for a brutal civil war in Athens, Greece, which was worse than anything the continent would experience for another fifty years or so.

German forces had banished Athens just six weeks ago, so now, Greek police and fragile British forces fought to maintain law and order in a city riddled with anguish and unhappiness. As soon as the sun rose, livid civilians snaked toward the city center. The police, as expected, tried to stop them from creating a ruckus, but the protestors, the majority of them women, caused the barricades put in their way to collapse and made their way through the central square, meeting on Premier George Papandreou's apartment building. The protestors, fuming in anger, marched into the building when a grenade exploded. George Papandreou remained hidden in his bedroom till his armed guards were able to usher the attackers back outside.

After some time, a crowd waving American, Soviet, Greek, and British flags gathered at the front of a police station. Unnerved and alarmed, the police withdrew until a man in uniform equipped with weapons ran out of the station and yelled, "Shoot the bastards!" He then threw himself down on one knee, opening fire on the crowd.

They followed the man, and in almost no time, the civilians collapsed, screaming. There were 12 dead and several wounded, while some others fled unharmed. British paras quietly watched the scenes playing in front of them, for they were ordered not to intercede. These histrionic events marked the end of three extremely long years of suffering for Greece. From 1941–1944, i.e., the Axis occupation of the country, nearly 100,000 people gave up their lives due to starvation. Resistance slowly began against Bulgarian, German, and Italian troops and interests.

In 1942, though, leftist radicals, including communists, Greek resistance groups, supporters of the ousted regime of Ioannis Metaxas, and other conservatives included, began battling each other as well as occupiers. Eventually, the communists merged with other groups into the National Liberation Front (EAM) and its tough National Popular Liberation Army (ELAS).

The EAM was rebutted by the Greek Government in exile, and so did the collaborationist government, which systematized, well-manned, and equipped security battalions. These forces received far higher casualties in anti-partisan operations than Italians or Germans.

The National Greek Republican League, also known as EDES, was another large resistance group of anti-communists, but it opposed the monarchist government in exile. The British secretly supported and provided for the EDES because it fought both the occupying forces and the EAM.

The British prime minister, Winston Churchill, began fearing in 1941 that Soviet developments in the Balkans would result in an EAM revolt and the setting up of a communist puppet regime. In a meeting on October 9 between Soviet premier Joseph Stalin and Churchill in Moscow, Churchill advised his counterpart.

Churchill offered to keep ninety percent of Greece and Stalin to keep ninety percent of Romania. Stalin nonchalantly agreed and stuck to the bargain.

Italy crumbled in the summer of 1943, and in September 1944, German forces began retreating from Greece. As they withdrew, anti-communist blocs got united to fight their mutual enemy. However, the better-synced and callous EAM, by the end of the year, had held control of most of Greece, excluding Crete.

In the meantime, the British forces prepared to occupy the main cities. Lieutenant General Ronald Scobie was placed in command of Force 140, a force of 10,000, by the Mediterranean commander-in-chief, Sir Henry Maitland Wilson.

The Germans retreated slowly but left behind an undamaged supply, arming security battalion garrisons, hoping to provoke civil war. By the time the Germans left Athens on October 12, the civil fight had already begun. British troops marched through the city two days later with Papandreou at their head.

Grieving of the evident Soviet support, the EAM got engaged in waves of compromise with the British, but it shortly broke faith, meting out propaganda, increasing conflict, and founding armed cells. At the beginning of December, open fighting between anti-communists and ELAS forces took place.

The Greek Government's declaration of demobilization for partisan development across the country ignited protests leading to the invasion of Papandreou's apartment and the carnage in front of the police station in Constitution Square.

By December 3, full-fledged fighting seriously began throughout the country, wherein about 22,000 ELAS fighters fought double that number of government troops comprising ex-Greek army units that retreated from exile, former security battalion troops, and mixt anti-communist resistance bands.

Our village was now trying to recover from the ruins of four years of war and going through another war, a civil war. Most of the village houses were burned down, and the other half lay in ruins from many battles fought during the occupation.

The fleeing Nazis left almost every window in people's homes broken from machine gun fire, the outside walls were riddled with bullet holes, and people were too exhausted and too weak to start any repairs; the only thing they cared about was working their gardens and growing food to feed themselves and their families.

Some homes were too dangerous to live in as they were structurally damaged from mortar or bazooka shelling that had holes the size of a soccer ball or larger going through from one side of the house and out the other.

Removing and disposing of decaying dead bodies lying on the side of the roads or dumped inside people's gardens, the villager's dogs starving like their masters were feasting on dead bodies or domestic dead animals.

Now, the villagers were able to work their farms and grow food for their families for the first time since the occupation, and our entire family started the cultivation of our farms which had been dormant for four years, and a new life for all the occupied people began.

However, the Andartes' war with the Greek Army was accelerating with intense fighting and heavy casualties, but at least the Nazi occupation was over, and hopefully, the civil war would be over soon. We hoped!!

In the meantime, my mother was pregnant and getting close to delivering her fourth child. I am not sure if they planned for another child; I didn't know much about those things at the time. I remember coming home from the fields one evening after a long, tiring day working in the fields. I was walking behind Truman, next to my brother, and we were talking about our family issues. In the heat of the moment, he told me something that came as a shock for me. He said, "Our mother is pregnant."

I was about eight years old at the time and was kind of shocked as nobody had told me that before. Once I was finally able to wrap my head around the fact that my mother was pregnant, I had a question for my brother. Why did our parents decide to have another baby now?

He was trying to make up a story but then ended up saying, "I think it was an accident."

His answer generated more questions for me, but I was tired and hungry and didn't have the energy to ask any more questions, so I continued walking our long walk back home, trailing behind Truman.

A few weeks later, I remember my mother sent me to stay a few days over at her sister's house. "Why?" I would ask everyone around me but to no avail. Of course, I later learned she was delivering a new baby in the house by a midwife named *Mami*. This was how most babies were delivered in our village and most villages around the country those days. Hospitals were not available in villages; they were only there in big cities (for obvious reasons).

I had to go to Sparta Hospital when I had my appendix removed, which I will never forget. The doctors gave me local anesthesia, and I was awake during the operation, yelling "*PONAO*," meaning, 'I am in pain.'

The doctor said to the nurse, "Give him something to eat." He thought I was hungry because the word '*PONO*' (I am in pain) rhymes with the word '*PINAO*,' which means "I am hungry."

The doctors made a joke out of me. They didn't have proper medication for me, the patient, but fortunately, I survived another example of torture in my young life.

This is me after my appendix surgery.

Chapter 7:

The Origins of the Civil War

Life was difficult for all of us after the German occupation and the consequential starvation. We went back to plowing the fields, *Horafia*, which we called "Vambakies." This was the name of the region our farm was in; we could now produce the food we needed to survive after four years of starvation. We tried to put back our broken lives and learn how to live normally again—without fear of being tortured or shot—unaware of what was coming next.

It was 1945. I was now nine years old with the dreadful German occupation behind us. We were looking forward to resuming our lives and perhaps repairing the wounds that the brutal Nazi murderers had afflicted upon us. The Greek resistance - known as the andartes that fought the Nazis for four years - had now turned their fight toward the weak Greek Army with the support of the eastern communist bloc.

There were two major guerilla commands operating out of our two regional mountains in our region of Peloponisus: one in our north named *Parnona* with the guerilla commander *Prekezes* and his fighters, and the other in the south on mount *Taygetos* near Sparta, which Kontaloni commanded. Both mountains were visible from our house, and we could hear and see the machine gun flashes at night when the andartes were fighting the Greek Army.

There was also a right-wing faction called *Hites;* it was a brutal bunch of killers masquerading as the defenders of the people of Peloponnesus from the andartes, which gave them free rein to kill thousands of innocent civilians and Greek soldiers in Peloponisus.

The Hites would come to our village, and the first thing they wanted to know was if the andartes (the Greek guerrillas) were still in the village. If they didn't like the answer, the villager who gave that answer would be shot dead and left on the ground for other villagers to pick up and bury.

We often found dead bodies among the wheat or corn fields. We could not ask who they were or how they were killed. We would just bury them in shallow graves out in the fields.

The weak, ill-equipped, and starved Greek Army fought many battles with the andartes near our house as they were trying to push them out and take control of our village. They had a post on top of the hill above our house, and I used to visit them as I did with the Germans not too long ago.

Five years later, I was doing the same thing, but this time, these soldiers were not Nazis; they were Greeks. We spoke the same language. It was sad for a nine-year-old to live through such an ordeal twice in such a short span of time.

Unlike the Nazis, who were well-fed and well-equipped soldiers, the Greek soldiers were poor boys who grew up during the occupation. The government now drafted them to fight and kill Greeks who used to kill Nazis. It was indeed a sad human tragedy, hard to comprehend by a young boy who grew up in one brutal war and now getting into another.

On the rare days when my mother had extra food, she would send me up to the post with some roasted potatoes or one loaf of bread and some Greek feta cheese, a favorite Greek food that made them feel good about being chosen to fight for their poor, war-torn country.

I watched them training in the event of an attack by the andartes, rolling down the hill with their weapon clutched to their chest until they found cover and then called for reinforcement. However, in my young eyes, they seemed to be a bit slow in executing the exercise. But what did I know about warfare? Only by watching the Nazis doing it with speed and precision, I became sure our guys could do it better with more and better training.

One day, there was a major battle beyond that rocky hill about two miles north of us, and these soldiers were now taking the fight to the andartes. We could visually see and hear the machine gun fire and stray bullets whizzing over our heads.

Many times, especially after bitterly fought battles, the andartes would raid the village looking for food, clothing, shoes, and medical supplies. I watched them bandage their wounded bodies in front of us.

This one time, while we were at "*Litrivio*," the olive processing plant, a group of armed andartes guerillas showed up with their guns drawn.

They said to us, "Take off your boots, pile them up in a designated area, and then stand in line to get paid for the boots."

I got 20 drachmas for my boots, and I had to walk home barefoot—not a first!

In 1947, two years after WWII ended, most villagers had lost everything, including mules, to work the fields and grow their food as they did before the occupation. The Greeks in America responded to our desperation and tried to help us help ourselves by sending us mules to plow our fields. The farms that had been growing weeds for the past five years instead of wheat, corn, potatoes, and other eating vegetables to feed our families could now be cultivated again. Those farms would now grow the food to help us heal some of the many wounds afflicted by the Nazis.

Like many other Greek relatives, my mother's brother, Uncle Gus, came to our rescue again by shipping us two huge mules. They landed in the port of Gythio, located on the other side of Mount Tayetus, a port town on the Southern Peloponisus that was a day's bus journey from our village.

My father was notified that he had to travel to Gythio to accept the delivery of the mules and bring them home because they didn't have the facilities to hold them for too long.

At the time, the town of Gythio was infested with Hites, a far-right group of bandits that were killing people for fun. After my father returned with the mules, he told us what had happened to him during his visit to Gythio.

When he arrived at the port to take delivery of the mules, he was met by a dozen Hites with their guns drawn. They asked him, "Are you harboring andartes back home?" He replied, "No way. I hate andartes."

The Hites said, "We don't believe you at all."

They wanted to have some fun. With a revolver pointed to his head, they laughingly ordered him, "Sing and dance the Greek Jembekiko." (Greek Jembekiko is a favorite Greek dance).

My father was neither a singer nor a dancer. However, he was now facing a bunch of bandits, well-known as murderers who killed for fun. With machine guns and pistols pointed at him, he sang and danced to save his life and bring the badly needed mules home.

One day, I woke up and saw two huge mules eating hay in our Avli Courtyard. I was never told how he transported them to our house. One mule was black, and the other was brown; both were unlike any mules I had ever seen. They were not at all like the small-bodied Greek mules; in fact, they were huge and wild. We had no idea if we could train them, put a saddle (*samari*) on them to ride or plow the fields.

These mules were so wild that when my little brother walked close to the black mule, he was sent flying with a strong kick. Although he landed about fifteen feet against a stone wall, he, fortunately, survived and recovered. This was not the last time he came close to death, though.

After that incident, and because this mule was not tamable, we thought it was not useful for us. My father said, "We should sell it and keep the brown one." Later, the brown one became the family workhorse. This mule helped us survive and get back on our feet. It replaced the old horse the Nazis took with them when they withdrew from our village.

Since we liked this mule, I suggested, "Hey, we should name this mule."

"Good idea." All agreed. "What should we name him?"

We all agreed on the name Truman after President Truman, a Greek hero who helped us defeat the guerillas and kept us from being taken over by the communists.

It didn't take long for Truman to be domesticated. After many incidents like throwing my mother off its *samari* that injured her back and almost killed my sister, he finally settled down. He then became a great working mule and a very close friend of mine.

One day, coming home at the end of a laborious day at the fields loaded with potatoes and other farm goods, Truman was calmly trotting in front of me. Suddenly, he jumped as a small animal crossed his path. Then, he started galloping down the dry riverbed until his load overturned, and he could not run anymore. He stood there waiting for me to help him.

I approached and consoled him first. "Don't worry, friend. Let me help you."

I unloaded him, turned the *samari* back on him, and tightened it hard around his belly, so it could not overturn easily. I reloaded him and said to him in Greek, "Do not do this again, my friend."

As expected, he repeated this a few more times until he got used to other animals running around him, both on the farm and at home.

After this episode, we continued our journey home, where my mother was waiting for me to eat my dinner of *trahana* or hilopites She asked with grave concern, "Why took you so long everything ok?" I told her what happened.

The civil war was still ongoing, and there were no signs of the war's end, especially in the northern part of Greece, close to the Albanian border. So many lives had been lost there. In our region, Peloponnesus, the guerillas were operating from the two major mountains, Mount Taygetus in the south and Mount Parnonas in the north, only a few hours from my village. That's where they would retreat after a major battle in their region, and there were many bloody battles.

Chapter 8:

Full Scale of the Greek Civil War

The Communist Party of Greece (KKE), a Marxist-Leninist organization, did not participate in the Greek elections of March 1946. With Civil War looming, they were forced to organize armed resistance in collaboration with ex-ELAS partisans, or *andartes*, by forming the Democratic Army of Greece (DSE). The new guerilla force was coordinated by resistance members from the safety of KKE-controlled hideouts in the mountains near the Albanian and Yugoslav borders. By the end of the year, they had made serious headway in much of rural Greece, and after the DSE attempted to wrest control of the city of Konitsa from the Greek National Army, the Communist Party itself was declared illegal.

Assisted by their communist neighbors (barring the notable exception of the Soviets themselves, who flirted with supporting the guerillas without ever truly committing to it), the KKE were able to establish their own provisional government based on Mt. Vitse and demand immense military and economic support from the United States. At the height of their success, they penetrated as far as Attica, only 20 kilometers from Athens.

Unfortunately for the communist resistance, the Allies supported the Kingdom of Greece, i.e., Athens, against them, with the US stepping in to fill the gap when the British could no longer deliver on the help they had pledged. With the Allies' support and being bolstered by the demoralizing effects of the Tito-Stalin split on communist morale, the Hellenic Army modernized and organized itself to finally defeat the guerillas, though not without a long, bitter struggle. This was the first proxy conflict between the Eastern and Western blocs, making it, in effect, the opening chapter of the Cold War.

Until then, however, the DSE used the logistical support and refuge offered by its communist allies to oppose the monarchy in several regions of Greece, most notably Peloponisus with the cooperation, or at least non-resistance, of the local population, which provided supplies to the guerillas when asked. By the spring of 1947, the DSE had been successful enough that much of rural Greece was under communist control—as much as seventy percent of Peloponisus under the DSE's III Division, as well as chunks of northeastern Greece, with battalions stationed on the islands of Lesvos, Lemnos, Ikaria, Samos, Creta, Evvoia, and most of the Ionian islands.

In response, the Western Allies went on pouring money, armaments, personnel, and other resources into Greece on behalf of the recognized government. A number of major offensives were planned and carried out under Allied supervision and direction, but it was some time before these efforts met with any success. The Democratic Army was well-entrenched, and the mountains remained a stronghold for most of the war's duration.

The tide turned when the Greek government came down hard on "communist sympathizers"—anyone caught providing assistance to the rebels faced eviction and imprisonment. Another key tactic used to turn the local population against the DSE was the "scorched earth" method, employed on the advice of the Greek National Army's American advisers, in which villages in rural areas were evacuated under the (often, admittedly, false) pretext that they were the targets of an "imminent communist attack," and the villagers herded into fortified towns, which were under government control. The consequent loss of homes and livelihoods soured villagers' attitudes toward the DSE and, more importantly, made it impossible for them to go on providing the guerillas with supplies and recruits.

This was the state of things in rural areas, but in the cities, the situation looked very different. Here, the EAM lacked support, and EAM members, ELAS partisans, and any communist or communist-sympathizing citizens were liable to be imprisoned on the island of Makronisos, labeled as traitors, or sentenced to death by firing squad for "crimes against the state." Exact figures are difficult to come by, but the number of Greek citizens who received capital punishment in this period totaling in thousands.

The summer of 1948 saw several major setbacks for the DSE, each following swiftly on the heels of the last. News of the Tito-Stalin split had arrived, and the KKE had to choose to cut ties with one or the other. It chose Stalin and the Soviets, but this, of course, alienated those who favored Tito, which led to a chaotic and destabilizing witch-hunt within the ranks of Greek Communism, causing the Party to lose support in urban areas. Moreover, the turn away from Tito meant the DSE could no longer access their Yugoslav refuges, Tito having disbanded their camps on Yugoslav soil. The Albanian border territories were still available, but they were no replacement for the safety to be found under Tito's shadow.

To make matters worse, the DSE's Division III suffered its worst-ever defeat, in which nearly all of a 20,000-strong force was wiped out by the Greek National Army. It was no contest; the communists were woefully under-supplied with ammunition from DSE headquarters after failing in its plan to capture weapons depots in Zacharo, in the western Peloponnese.

By the end of 1948, resistance in the Peloponisus had collapsed; the region was in the hands of paramilitary groups that fought alongside the Army; only rural Greek Macedonia and Epirus remained in the hands of the KKE's provisional government. In a renewal of the atrocities of the White Terror, pro-Kingdom forces swept across the country. The EAM, anticipating direct attacks on areas under their control, evacuated women, children, the old, and the infirm to Albania. From Albania, the refugees traveled to Yugoslavia, which had closed its borders with Greece. Despite this, Slav Macedonian fighters continued to join DSE ranks, although the cause was, by this point, effectively lost.

Meanwhile, the Western Allies continued to pour money, armaments, and personnel into Greece on behalf of the royalist cause. A series of heavy defeats in the islands and the Peloponisus, an ill-fated attempt to take over the city of Konitsa, and the abandonment of Macedonia by locals in what came to be known as the Macedonian Exodus led to the swift destabilization of the DSE in the first half of 1949. Soviet support, too, had been withdrawn, with Stalin referring disparagingly to the communist resistance in Greece as merely a "Greek uprising." When asked what the Greek Communists should do, Stalin replied, *"Svernut,"* which is Russian for "fold up."

For its part, the Greek National Army was not shy about subduing the formerly DSE-controlled regions, even going so far as to destroy the Kastorian village of Pimenikon by bombing it from the air. Prison camps were set up in Ikaria, Makronisos, Thessaloniki, Larisa, and Athens; there, communist fighters and sympathizers, along with countless displaced families, suffered the privations of hunger, malnutrition, sickness, and injury, not to mention torture, punitive labor, and executions. While the precise numbers are hotly disputed, with estimates for the total number of refugees ranging from 30,000 to as many as 213,000, it is indisputable that tens of thousands of noncombatant people were displaced.

Thousands of refugees were on the move, crossing the border into Albania and Yugoslavia. Younger women joined the partisans remaining in the mountain holdouts, while the older women accompanied the children and helped them across the border. The widows of fallen resistance fighters became surrogate mothers for children whose mothers had been killed or were hiding out with their husbands.

About a thousand DSE fighters had fled from Greece by the end of September 1949. The Communist Party of Greece no longer had any foothold on home soil; now displaced, the DSE had to relocate to new headquarters in Tashkent, in the Soviet Union. For the next three years, they would live in military barracks. Noncombatants (and older combatants, unfit for further conflict) such as women, children, and the sick and injured were resettled in various European socialist countries that were willing to accept them. Greek Communism did not die, but there was no longer any armed resistance to speak of.

Having watched the real battles between the andartes and the government forces, we now wanted to play fake battles among ourselves. The days of playing with little glass balls on the streets were over; now, we were into playing dangerous war games between groups dressed in red or white, using homemade handguns that did not fire bullets—at least, not yet—but pretending they were real guns.

Our parents were very worried about us being kidnapped, like the thousands of children that had been taken to Albania and Bulgaria to be part of the Communist bloc. They discouraged us from walking on the streets alone.

There was a group of about six kids from the village, all around the same age, who played these games of pretend warfare, one side playing the andartes and the other playing Greek soldiers. We used sticks for guns, laid ambushes for each other, and engaged in fierce mock skirmishes. Some crafty kids carved handguns out of wood that looked very much like the real thing. These were prized objects.

After some time, one particularly crafty kid, too clever for his own good, was able to build a crude but dangerous homemade handgun designed to fire small pellets like a shotgun. He accomplished this by cutting a 10-inch piece of metal pipe out of an old bed frame; this was the gun barrel. Then he flattened and folded one side of the pipe to hold the powder and made a small hole on top through which to ignite it. The pipe, or rather the barrel, fit tightly into a channel on the handcrafted stock and was secured with bare wire.

Of course, he wanted to demonstrate his invention to us. He claimed he could load—and what was more, actually fire—his new handgun with small lead pellets scavenged from an unexploded cartridge. How did he get his hands on live ammunition? It was simple; anybody could do so. It was everywhere; rifle and shotgun cartridges could be found lying on the ground, particularly in villages like ours, where there had been fighting in the immediate vicinity. After a battle, we kids would go scrounging around, looking for unexploded munitions from rifle cartridges, hand grenades, mortar shells, or anything else explosive. For us, these things were just a better class of toy—one that would let us get closer, in our play, to what the soldiers and andartes were doing around us.

So, there we were, standing around on a patch of bare ground just outside the village, waiting for this gun inventor to show us the best weapon any of us had made.

"Stand back!" he said. "Back!"

Reluctantly, we withdrew to what we thought was a safe distance. The question of what would keep the inventor himself safe did not occur to us.

"And cover your ears," he added, though, of course, he was far closer to the source of the sound than we, and he couldn't cover his ears at all, his hands being occupied with the gun and the cigarette lighter he would use to fire it.

We had no idea what would happen. On the one hand, there was an undeniable attraction about the gun he had made, and we were all longing to get our hands on it. On the other, we had seen kids playing with high-grade military gunpowder before, and when they did, things tended to explode.

The tension was very high with all of us, including the gunsmith. With the gun in his left hand and the lighter in his right, he flicked the little flame to life, then lowered it carefully toward the small hole at the end of the barrel closest to him.

"Kaboom!"

There was a tremendous, ear-splitting bang, sending all of us diving for cover. The air was filled with hot smoke. When the cloud had cleared, we saw the inventor standing there, still holding the gun stock, minus the barrel—it was blown into small pieces, some of which were found several meters away. Thankfully, we were lucky, and none of them had pierced an eye or embedded itself in someone's skin. You can imagine what a shard of metal pipe could do to a person, moving through the air at such speed.

We all stood there speechless, our mouths hanging open. The great craftsman—incredibly—was unhurt. A couple of kids were running home, dying to tell their mothers what had just happened. The rest of us, stunned by what we had just witnessed—not least the gun's designer—were thinking about how many kids had been killed playing with live ammunition. We were aware we could easily have joined them; we had taken it too far.

One positive thing came out of this bad experience—it put an end to the production of handmade handguns among our group. Others persisted, though. They went on to find steel pipes that could withstand small explosions, loaded them up with pellets, and went about killing animals on the streets until the end of the war, when it was forbidden to make or use handmade guns.

The roads and fields were filled with live munitions from recent battles between the andartes and the Army and sometimes between andartes and Chites ("Organization X," a right-wing, anti-communist, royalist paramilitary group). Many young kids were killed playing with these things they thought were toys that blew up in their faces.

For a long time, not a single day went by without news of some kid who was killed playing with live ammunition. Ultimately, the villagers set up a mandatory program to teach the kids how to recognize the various types of ammunition and not to touch them but, instead, notify an adult or a policeman and never, ever play with them. As a result, the frequency of deaths was reduced, but they were not entirely eliminated until a few years after the end of the civil war when discarded munitions were no longer plentiful.

It is understandable that we, the kids who had grown up under the occupation of a cruel and savage enemy that tortured and killed thousands of innocent people and were now living through a cruel and devastating civil war, would be fascinated with guns, bombs, and violence. The warfare all around us served as a daily dose of survival lessons, and it taught us very different things from what children ought to be learning; it was not an education, and it did not prepare young people to become useful members of their community or society.

Unfortunately, during that sad passage of history, millions of kids like us all over the world were robbed of the opportunity of education, which was denied to them by a vicious enemy in the form of the Nazis, whose quest for world domination brought us the civil war.

I lived through this gruesome war, and in the course of it, I witnessed many battles between the andartes and the Greek soldiers. They were the ones keeping the andartes away; whatever our loyalties, the soldiers were, in some sense, our protectors, and we wanted to stay on their good side.

One bright morning, we woke up to the sound of stray machine gun bullets whizzing over our house. Then, suddenly, we heard someone cry, "Look out! Mortar shell!" A heartbeat later, there was an explosion not far from us; it shook the house, rattling the furniture, and we felt the vibrations come up through the ground and into our bodies, which we had dropped to the ground upon hearing the voice cry, "Shell!"

But there was no time to take in what had just happened. We heard loud screams coming from the top of the hill, so we ran to see what had happened and found a neighbor lying on the ground, bleeding from his neck and screaming for help. Someone else was trying to stop the bleeding.

"What happened?" I asked, not able to comprehend this thing I'd seen so often in our pretend war games.

"He was hit by a stray bullet," the man who was trying to stop the blood said. "Why are you outside? Get indoors!"

I ran back to our house and told my mother what had happened up on the hill. She told everyone to get inside the house to avoid being injured or killed by stray bullets. We did so, but the telltale whine of the bullets could still be heard as they passed through the air above the village or landed in it. The streets were empty. Everyone was indoors.

Soon after, however, we saw all our neighbors coming out of their homes and walking up the hill to see where all these stray bullets were coming from. We soon joined them; there was a major battle going on straight ahead, about a thousand yards up on a hill, and the people of our village were watching it.

Not only could we hear the machine-gun fire; we could also see the gun flashes, mortar and hand-grenade explosions, soldiers running and taking cover, plumes of black smoke rising after mortar blasts, and flames of burning brush and small trees called "pournaria" (a thorny tree with small green leaves that can cause injuries if touched or fall into it), found near or in forests.

We could hear the women crying and sobbing as they watched soldiers (sons, brothers, or fathers) getting killed. More than two hours later, the gunfire stopped, and we began to see soldiers moving around the battlefield, removing their dead and wounded as well as the fallen andartes—as proof of how many they had killed. Those andartes that survived the fierce battle managed to escape into the forest to recuperate, some of them living to fight the next battle.

As we watched the fighting, most of us had tears in our eyes; we were watching the tragedy of Greeks killing Greeks, not Greeks killing Germans, as it was during the Occupation. Most people could not bear the pain of watching and went home to cry alone. Only a few of us were left, standing there and waiting for the Greek soldiers to pass by on their way back to their headquarters.

What my friends and I did not expect to see was what our soldiers were carrying with them. It was the most gruesome sight we had ever seen with our innocent young eyes: nine headless bodies, riddled with bullets, disfigured beyond recognition—the bodies of slain andartes, carried on ladders like dead baggage, and their heads in sacks like watermelons.

I can still remember the sounds made by the crying, sobbing women who couldn't bear the pain and sorrow of seeing fellow human beings, regardless of their ideology, with bodies torn apart like animals' bodies, being carried to the village square for display.

It was a gruesome sight for a 9-year-old, and there were children much younger than me, all watching, speechless, holding their mothers' hands, seeing the horrific images of human beings' dismembered bodies. How can I forget such horrible images? They are permanently set in stone, burned into my brain, and, to this day, they are still lodged there; they will remain there till the day I die.

I remember, one day, about a dozen andartes came to our house after a bitter battle with the Germans. Badly wounded and hungry, they were looking for any medical assistance that our parents could provide to heal their bullet wounds and broken bones. They had a woman *andartisa* with them; she seemed to be a trained nurse, and I watched her trying to stop the bleeding from various wounds. She was overwhelmed by all the wounded people around her, so she asked my mother, "Ma'am, please help us."

Some of the andartes had serious wounds like broken bones missing arms and bullet holes in the chest that she could treat. I saw one *andarti* whose leg was riddled with bullet holes; the blood was gushing out all over our floor.

Another man's arm was missing below the elbow; he was crying for help.

Another was groaning in excruciating pain; his hands were clasped over the open wound in his belly.

This was like a nightmare for me; I couldn't believe my eyes. I was watching grown men crying and screaming from pain, begging for help. We all wanted to help them, but our house was not a hospital with doctors and medicine to treat their wounds and stop their pain; it was just our house, and the war had put these men and their suffering inside it.

We did not have enough space to keep them, so some of the wounded were put in my bedroom, where the andartisa nurse ministered to them with my mother's help. There was no proper medicine. Many times, she literally yelled at my mother, "You've got to do more to help us."

Well, her shouting was of no use because my mother was not a nurse. I suppose the woman must have been desperate. And who could blame her?

My mother did the best she could to stop the bleeding of the wounded. She used our clothes to control the blood flow, and still the floor was covered in it. So was she. Her hands, her arms, her dress, her neck, her face—all, all were swathed in the andartes' scarlet blood.

I was watching her; she looked desperate. Then, there came a moment when our eyes met, and I could see something happening in her eyes as she saw me for the first time, standing in the corner of my bedroom, applying pressure to a wounded man's blood-soaked arm with a rag I had torn from the tablecloth.

My mother crossed the room to where I stood and gently took my place, her hands substituting for mine without releasing the pressure.

"Go out onto the terrace," she said in a low voice, "and stay there till I come out."

She didn't want me to see what was going on in that room and remember those horrific images for the rest of my life, but it was too late for me to ever forget what I had seen that night.

I did what my mother told me to do: I walked out onto the terrace and sat down, leaning against the stone wall, sobbing about what I had witnessed. When I finally raised my head and opened my eyes, I saw that I was sitting next to two machine guns with their magazines loaded, facing out toward the village, and I wanted to know how it felt to sit behind a Bren (a British machine gun).

I lay down behind it and pretended I was in a battle, mimicking the sounds of gunfire. Soon, I noticed a handle sticking out on the right side of the gun. I was curious about the function of this handle, and I tried to pull it back, but it was hard to hold, so I let it go. The clinking sound was heard by the andartes inside the house, and suddenly, before I could pull the trigger, a strange hand had taken a fierce grip on my ear, and I was being dragged bodily away from the machine gun. One of the andartes was shouting at me.

"I just wanted to know how it feels!" I pleaded; the pain in my ear felt sharp and hot.

"Never touch the guns again!" the man said in a stern tone. "You just cocked this thing. It's ready to fire."

He let go of my ear, then removed the loaded magazine and removed the shell from the chamber.

"Stay inside the house," he said in a calmer tone. "Help your mother to clean the men's wounds."

This was another incident of playing with real guns; this time, it didn't cause any injuries or deaths, but it had the potential of doing both. They told my mother what I had done, and after she had scolded me, she took me to a bed she had made up for me in another room.

"Go to sleep," she said. "Don't touch anything of theirs again."

And she shut the door and was gone.

I was very tired and mad at myself for doing such a stupid thing; then I pulled my blanket over my head and cried until I fell asleep, and for me, this miserable day was over.

The next day, when I woke up, everyone was gone, including all the guns out on the terrace. Only the bloody rags and floor from their wounds and the horrible memories of the wounded and groaning men were left behind.

On October 16, 1949, the Greek communist broadcasting station—Radio Free Greece—announced the end of open hostilities, and many of the remaining communist fighters fled the country into neighboring Albania.

Chapter 9:

Life Under the Civil War

Life under the communist guerillas was just as difficult and bitter as it was during the four years of Nazi occupation. Killings and atrocities committed by guerillas became a normal part of life, but at the same time, we were finally able to work the farms and avoid starvation.

It was common for us to witness murders of family members, friends, and neighbors and vicious, bloody battles between communists and royalists in the village and surrounding areas. When one of our neighbors found out that his next-door neighbor was a royalist who didn't agree with communism, he shot and killed him with his shotgun.

Over the course of the five years of civil war, the village was torn apart by two fatal ideologies, and the number of casualties and hardships increased dramatically. Many battles and senseless killings were constantly fought in our village and neighborhood between various Guerilla bands and a new far right-wing faction called 'Hites,' who opposed the Guerrillas.

As the civil war raged on, the KKE (Greek Communist Party), in collaboration with the communist Eastern bloc countries, was planning to deliver Greece to the communist Russians. The bloodiest and most horrific battles between the Guerrillas and the Greek Army took place in Northern

Greece near the Albanian and Bulgarian borders, where all the border villages were the hardest hit by the Guerrillas.

Ilia (Olive Tree) was the name of one of those border villages. Its name was born by a settler who attempted to cultivate an olive tree, bringing a sapling from the valley with him to the arid uplands. Although legend has it that the tree didn't live very long, the new settlers proudly proclaimed, "We are going near Ilia, the olive tree." It was perched precariously on a cliff face in northwest Greece, not far from the Albanian border, and directly beneath the upper slopes of the Mourgana mountain range. All that remains of the bloodshed that occurred here during the last German occupation and the Greek civil war is a village.

A Brief History of the Invaders of Northern Greece
The Ottomans

In the 15th century, after the Turks conquered Greece, the people of Ilia began to return to the mountains to avoid persecution. It became increasingly difficult for the villagers to get to higher ground as the Turks made more kidnappings of young men and boys for their Elite Corps, as well as girls for their harems. These mountains are now home to five villages that are roughly a half-walk hour from one another.

There were few Turkish raids in these high altitudes during the 400-year occupation of the Ottoman Empire from 1430 to 1912, but occasionally, the representatives of the pasha of the region would come to collect taxes. A kerchief tied around the neck of any woman venturing out during these times was a requirement for any woman venturing out at all. In Turkish style, the men wore black pantaloons gathered at the knees over black socks and composed of shoes, a white shirt, and a square vest, often embroidered. Some also wore the traditional fez headdress.

The Nazis

The Nazis made the town of Ioannina their headquarters in Northern Greece in 1943, and bands like EAM and EDES of Guerillas were formed in the rugged country around the village of Ilia. As time went on, the Skives brothers, both Communists, took control of EAM, making it more and more left-wing. However, Ilia's villagers were split over which party to vote for, although the town's left-wing EAM was the overwhelming choice.

When the Nazis arrived in 1943 from the south, three men from our community, who had no idea the Nazis were coming, ran into a Nazi patrol and were killed instantly with machine gun fire. Then they dragged their bodies to the edge of the road and dumped them over a deep cliff.

They continued their march into the village of Babouri, where the villagers decided to use a German-speaking woman to appeal to the Nazi commander not to burn down their village, and as a result, the village was spared, but they burned down the next two villages.

The Communist Guerillas

After the Nazi defeat (they eventually left in 1944), the Guerillas took the lessons learned by the Nazis and occupied almost all the villages near the Albanian border and made the lives of the people of Northern Greece hell on Earth.

Ilia's food supply was becoming increasingly scarce. It was a two-day journey by mule to Igoumenitsa on the Ionian Sea, and some villagers, particularly women, took on the hard work of providing food for their families. They would ride their mules and travel through mountains to reach a desert where they would fill large sacks of salt loaded on the mules and their backs and return to the village., Then climb over the mountain's summit into Albania, where they would exchange salt for corn with the land-locked Albanians.

Women who were weak from hunger did this even in the dead of winter. In 1942, as she descended from the Albanian border, one woman became lost in the snow. It was not until the following spring that the body of this young woman was discovered.

Other villagers gave the guerillas the impression that the men of Ilia were eager to join the Communist cause. It was shocking to discover that the village was entirely made up of women and children when the invading guerrillas first arrived. After the guerillas made themselves at home, they established defenses, seized food, and forced the women to work for them. As the months went by, the Communists grew angrier and more brutal in their attacks on Greek Army units. Despite some initial success, they were losing many fighters and began recruiting young girls to fight.

Many family members were tried and executed by the guerillas for opposing their cause and ideology, and in public trials, the family members of those accused of opposing the EAM policy were required to testify against them to save their own lives. Children were forced to watch their parents die. It was common for dead bodies to remain in the town square for days on end. The EAM Guerillas resembled the Nazis in how they treated the Greek people during the occupation and repeated their actions in every respect.

The communists' headquarters was in the largest house in the village, where they kept prisoners in the basement. Other executed prisoners were buried in the front yard or stuffed into a well. The guerrillas executed five to ten people in every village they occupied, regardless of whether there were any escape attempts. By making residents testify against each other, the Communists hoped to scare the villagers into submission.

It was common for the women of the village, young and old, to be sent into the battle zone to assist the troops by carrying the wounded, digging graves, and performing other duties. The guerrillas began gathering women for a work crew the day before the intended escape, on June 24th, 1948. One out of every two women over the age of 13 was required to go to the wheat fields and harvest and thresh grain for the soldiers. On this day, each family was required to supply up to two women from that age group.

Compared to the villages to the east and west, Ilia has the advantage of being situated in an indentation where the mountain's slope is more gently declining. Barbour, the next village to the west, is perched dangerously on the edge of a sheer cliff face. It looks like an arena; the houses are built on stilts and stacked one on top of the other, with thick stone walls in between them.

Boys who were eight years old or above helped their fathers around the house and farm hand with chores like gardening, milking the sheep and goats, spinning wool, weaving cloth, cutting brushwood, and cooking.

In Ilia, most men worked in one of three main trades, the top one being tin smithing. There were long journeys undertaken by the Tinsmiths that would keep them away for six months to a year. They made their way from town to town, stopping at each residence to see if pots needed to be cleaned, mended, or replaced with the new ones they brought along with them. Cooking utensils were always scorched black because everyone cooked over an open fire. The tinkers were sent to scrub the huge pots' exteriors. The small boys were responsible for cleaning the inside of the house.

The pots were first filled with sand and water, followed by animal skin; the boys would stand in the pot and scour it with their feet until it was shiny. Tinkers were known to connive and steal in Greece and send their children to beg in people's homes. However, the tinkers of Ilia took great pride in their well-deserved good name among their peers.

The second on the list were coopers. The coopers in Ilia would make wooden kegs, barrels, vats, buckets, and other similar containers out of timber staves. The cooper would be a well-trained individual in this field; to make the items pliable, they would steam or heat staves (a narrow piece of wood with a slightly beveled edge used to form the sides of various containers, such as barrels, tanks, tubs, vats, and pipelines). For months or even years, coopers departed their homes to travel across Greece to build enormous wooden casks with a level of craftsmanship that is unmatched today. Milling was the third most common job; most of the population had to leave their homes to work as millers.

The Kidnapping of the Greek Children

Thousands of Greek children were taken from their homes by force and sent to communist countries to be indoctrinated into the communist ideology and eventually learn to hate their own country Greece. The Guerillas were trying to convince the mothers and the rest of the Greek people that their actions were necessary to protect children from the horrors of war, as communist guerillas were in a war with the government forces and transported more than 25,000 children, mostly to Albania, Bulgaria, and Czechoslovakia.

Greek authorities, however, insisted that the Communist Party was simply trying to recruit more members for the sole purpose of seizing power once again. With funding from the Royal Fund, Greece's then-Queen Frederica established children's villages all over the country to protect young people from communists who might abduct them from the front lines. When the war ended in 1950, they were able to return home to their communities.

In order to justify sending children abroad, the Communist Party (KKE) claimed they had parental permission but failed to mention that most parents had already enlisted in the guerrilla army. Children of the Greek civil war were placed in children's homes in many communist countries, including the Asian providences of the Soviet Union.

These children were taken from their homes and sent to communist countries where they were forced to learn the communist language and ideology and took away their Greek citizenship and were socially, as well as religiously, isolated from their mother country where they were raised as Greek Orthodox Christians. For many, the chance to return to their homeland was once in a lifetime, but it was too late to change their minds about the country they were raised in, which they had all been taught to hate.

Moving Children Inside Albania

The guerillas decided to divide the children into groups with 'mothers' in charge because the government troops were advancing fast and were bombing all the villages near the Albanian border. Several hundred walked through the night until they came across these tiny bright lights, some of them who were only toddlers at the time.

The Albanian border guards' cigarette tips were the signal for them to cross the border. Once inside the communist countries, the children were raised and forced to become good communist fighters and return to Greece to live in a Greek communist country after they won the war; Greece would be a communist country like the one they were raised in and indoctrinated to be good communists.

In August 1949, Marshal "Alexander Papagos" launched a final national army offensive assisted by the Americans and forced the guerrillas to either surrender or flee across the northern border to communist countries. The civil war claimed the lives of more than 100,000 people and wreaked havoc on the country's economy.

The Exodus of Refugees

A group of fifty people, many of them children, gathered in the village's southernmost house as if for a social get-together. The children were instructed to play tag in a nearby cave. They were waiting for the adults to find them and take them to a hiding place. At night, they would go down the mountain, cross the hills, and climb up the next range until they met up with Greek Government Forces.

During the night and just after dawn, they walked, mostly barefoot, and found a Royalist unit that led them the final three miles to a road while awaiting the arrival of a government army truck. Women screamed when they saw the truck coming, and the Greek soldiers helped everyone onto the truck and started singing and laughing. It was a happy journey for everyone squeezed in an open army truck.

That was the beginning of a long journey for many refugees, which began with a two-day boat trip from Igoumenitsa on the Ionian Sea to Athens, where they were eventually placed on a refugee boat bound for the United States - thanks to the efforts of family members.

Ilia Became a Ghost Town

By the fall of 1948, Ilia had become a ghost town. There were some people that wanted to revive life as it was before the Guerilla occupation and returned, but most of the village's men opted to leave and join the post-war exodus from the rural areas, leaving behind their wives and children who had been left behind. In the early 50s, when the first refugees began to return across the border, the Greek Government offered them loans to rebuild their homes and villages.

The younger generation had enough of toiling to maintain a meager existence in Athens and decided to head to the United States in search of a better life. There are now only 180 people living in Ilia on a permanent basis. At its peak, Ilia had a population of 1,200 people, served by three mills, and worshipped in 11 churches, including the Aghia Panaghia, a centuries-old church (Church of Our Lady). Only one of the churches in the area is being used on a regular basis. Currently, all six students from the small town are housed in the large village school's single classroom. The remainder of the structure has been transformed into a vocational training center for young women from 16 nearby villages, where they can learn skills like cooking, sewing, and embroidery. However, in Ilia itself, young women are virtually nonexistent.

Elderly residents predominate, with most villagers being in their 60s or older. The village's way of life, despite advancements, remained primitive. Women used ancient agricultural methods to work the rocky soil. It's still a mystery how people handled indoor plumbing. When electricity arrived in 1965, it ushered in a new era in daily life for those living in the village, making it easier for them to communicate with others. The bouzouki music on the radios has now overpowered the tinkling of sheep bells. However, while many villagers still fetch water from the springs, others have installed pipes that funnel the water into a sink in the backyard.

The senior residents of Ilia rely on the road as a lifeline; it brings them money from their relatives who live in other countries, government pensions, and daily newspapers. For the first part of the journey from Filiates, a large town to the southwest of the Mourgana Range, the route ascends the mountains and follows an intricate route through the villages, often clinging to the top of cliffs, before descending from the mountains to Ioannina in Greece's southernmost region.

Nicholas Barkas' cafenion (outdoor cafe and grocery store) is the next establishment on the road. Panagiotis Bourakas isn't pleased when he sees more of the town's residents at his competitor's cafenion than his own. A gray-bearded priest who was once a cooper lives below the road at this point. He now serves as a liaison between the village and the villagers in Athens and the United States, informing them of the village's needs.

The road bisects the village square, which is known as ta Alonia because it is where the wheat is separated. A massive maple tree provides welcome shade to Kostas Vrenetis, the village president's brother's cafenion. Villagers can buy cigarettes, newspapers, toothpaste, stamps, aspirin, candy, and a dizzying array of other goods at the kiosk across from the cafenion. Disabled veterans typically receive concessions for these kiosks, which can be found all over Greece.

The church of the Holy Trinity, which sits below the square, was rebuilt thanks to the generosity of villagers from other countries. On Ilia's feast day, when throngs of worshippers ascend to the summit of the mountain for the services, Ilia often resembles its former self during the summer. After that, everyone heads to the dam's flat pasture above the village for a picnic. Roasted lambs are served with huge trays of cheese and spinach pie by the village women. Folk songs from Greece are played by Gypsies as they move between festivals in the region of Epirus, where the Tsamikos dance is popular.

Although Ilia shows signs of life every now and then, its death is imminent. There will be a few—if any—returnees on the feast day in the years to come, and it is just one of many Greek villages that have been thrown out of the country. It's impossible to predict what Greece would be like without these villages. The villages were Greece to most Greeks born in the first half of the twentieth century, whether they lived in Athens,

Johannesburg, Stuttgart, New York, or Rio. Their character and future were shaped by their upbringing in the small town. Most Greeks don't want to return to their hometowns, but they'll never forget their childhood memories, including the author of this piece.

There were only a few plots of land in Ilia that could be tilled, and they were scattered throughout the town. Those who owned the largest plots of land in the village had the highest social status in the community. It was the women's responsibility to cultivate the land, as well as to search the ravines for scrub brushwood and carry enormous amounts of it up the mountain. In these plots of land, corn was the best crop grown, and it was the source of cornbread.

Vegetables and cornbread were the staple foods of most of the villagers. To till the land, every family had a goat, donkey, or mule. Young girls were taught to help around the house and farm with chores like growing food, milking animals, spinning, and weaving yarn, cutting brushwood, cooking, and cleaning, while older boys assisted their fathers with household chores after the age of eight.

After the communist defeat by the Greek Army, they finally realized that their dream of a communist Greece was shattered and began to allow some of the refugees from Albania and other communist countries to return to Greece. Some who wanted to come back were not allowed in by the Greek Government because it was feared that they had become too indoctrinated and hated their own country. Other Greeks who had supported the guerrillas did not dare to return for fear of what their fellow villagers would do to them. Half of the refugees remain behind the iron curtain today.

These children, now adult men, now returning home to Greece, have already paid the price for their fathers' sins; these children are the innocent victims of the conflict. As a result, they have no idea who they are anymore when asked by Greek border guards about their Greek names and birth towns. Many were afraid they would be silenced forever if they tried to share their experiences. The Greek Government made this choice in the hopes that reintegrating these kids as adults would help the country move past the trauma of its civil war and into the modern era as a more inclusive and democratic place. Political refugees were now allowed to stay in Greece for up to 20 days as per the new decree.

After nine years of death and destruction, Greece once again was free from the Nazis and the communist occupation. Death and destruction began the lengthy recovery from the ashes to its full Democratic way of life. Our village also celebrated the end of communism in the village square, singing and dancing to the end of a lengthy tyranny that lasted for days.

Like young Ilia, we, too, here in my village, began the exodus to other democratic countries untouched by the Nazis and civil wars, seeking freedom, education, and jobs. America opened its doors to people who could provide proof of civil war affliction and have a sponsor in America. They could apply for a visa.

My mother jumped to this God-sent opportunity and wrote to her brother Gus in America to send me the required sponsorship papers so I could apply for my visa and have a chance to live a better life. As usual, he was there to help us all, and once again, he lost no time to answer our needs; I met all the qualifications required to immigrate to

America under the program designed to help people like me who were afflicted by the civil war.

Angelo Metropoulos, the author of *"The Wild and Twisted Branch: The Story of Stavros Metropoulos and how he Survived the Greek Civil War,"* tells the story of his father, Stavros. In this book, he recounts his father's incredible struggle to survive the German occupation and the Greek civil war and how he immigrated to America.

The Tom Fassas Story

Tom Fassas, now 94 years old, recalls his ordeals of growing up during the Nazi occupation and the Greek civil war. Tom was born and raised in a small village called "Agios Georgios" (St. George South) in Northern Greece. It is a picturesque village built on the side of a tall, rugged mountain, tacked away among thick green trees with a population of about 900 residents, all making a living working their farms and livestock of sheep and goats. Tom was the second oldest of three brothers, and they all worked on the farm helping their parents grow enough food to survive during the civil war. However, during the Nazi occupation, they were forbidden to work the farms because the Nazis took control of all the villagers' farms and livestock to feed their soldiers. Only if there were a surplus would they distribute it to the villagers. The Nazis used starvation to control the civilian population.

Even at this stage of his life, Tom recalls the unforgettable day when his village and house were set on fire by the Nazis and burned to ashes. He remembers watching the Nazis throwing flares on the roof of houses and witnessing two Nazis setting their home ablaze. He saw their house engulfed with hot red flames, and in minutes, it was turned to ashes.

The entire family was in utter shock watching the house their parents built while raising their three sons being consumed by flames and thick smoke. Tom could not forget seeing his father holding back his screaming mother from trying to run into her burning house to save their valuables, including the livestock, as they were burning. Desperation had taken over logic.

Tom thought he was having a nightmare, but he soon realized he was not dreaming. He watched the house he was born and raised in real-time disappear in front of his eyes. "The thick black toxic smoke rising from the smoldering flames and the stench of burning livestock was choking us and was hard to breathe."

"My father told us, 'There is nothing we can all do here. We must move away before we all collapse from this acrid environment'."

Fortunately, there were few houses still standing, and he noticed his brother Kosta's house up the hilltop, hidden behind tall trees was one of them.

In Tom's own words…

"Move fast to get there, my father cautioned. My older brother Nick and I were helping our sobbing mother to walk, following our father. He knocked on my brother's front door two times than once; it was their identification signal. The door opened; my brother peaked halfway through to ensure it wasn't the Nazis. He gasped when he saw us all depressed; my mother was still sobbing. He knew what had happened. I heard him asking my father, did they burn your house? My father shook his head up and down. Come into the house quickly, my uncle said, and he shut and locked the door behind us."

Tom was about 16 years old when the Nazis entered his village and began burning it to the ground as retribution for the death of two Nazi soldiers killed by the guerillas in an ambush nearby. This was a normal and expected Nazi reaction as they had warned all Greeks of the consequences when one of their soldiers was killed by the guerillas or a civilian. They would kill 50 civilians and burn the nearest village. So, this was retribution for the deaths of two Nazis killed by the guerillas in an ambush nearby.

Next to torture and shootings, hunger and famine were the two main causes of death for many villagers during the Nazi occupation. After the Nazis' defeat, the Greek civil war began, and the killings and human misery continued. Many battles were fought in and near my village between the Guerillas and the Greek army; only this time, the family could work the farms and avoid starvation. Where under the occupation, the Nazis had taken control of our farms and our livestock to feed their soldiers and forbade us to work the farms because starvation was a crucial part of controlling the civilian population. Tom recalls the suffering of hunger, sickness, and the daily fear of death for himself and his family. "Your mother does not have anything to cook for dinner, and she wanted you to go up the hills looking for sweet bulbs like onions growing underground so she could cook."

After the civil war ended in 1950, Tom was able to immigrate to America in 1956. He worked hard in the construction business, married the love of his life, Phyllis, from Connecticut, and together they raised two wonderful children, Randy and Christine, and lived the American dream. Tom and I came to America simultaneously, but it took us more than 30 years to meet and become great neighbors and great friends. I met Tom when we moved to his neighborhood. During our family gatherings at his house or ours, we always ended the day with stories about our lives during the Nazi occupation and the Greek civil war.

The Greek civil war was a dark cloud in Greek history. It was a fight for the survival of democracy in Greece and around the world. There was one man who saved Greece from becoming part of the communist bloc: American President Harry S. Truman.

Chapter 10:
Civil War Atrocities

These are some of the communist Guerilla atrocities.

One of the worst and most outrageous massacres was the Meligalas Massacre at the village of Meligalas in the southern region of Messinia, a region of Peloponnesus. It became the site of one of the darkest pages in Greek history. A somber memorial of 887 crosses with the names of the civilians murdered by EAM - ELAS guerillas—a bitter battle between ELAS and the collaborationists.

Eyewitness, official, and popular stories of what transpired next are numerous, and they typically differ depending on whose side they came from. The local communist guerillas are widely believed to have carried out the first round of retaliation, starting with the summary execution of enemies they identified among the surrendered: a gendarme here, a known collaborator there. Then, villagers from nearby regions arrived. Having endured hardships and executions because of the occupation from both the Germans and the Security Battalions, they descended on the liberated village and started exacting further retribution by burning, looting, and killing more prisoners - helped by the guerillas' purposefully lax attitude towards the safety of the surrendered. A summary court was established around September 15th, and mock trials started to involve the people of Meligalas and the nearby villages, men, and women, young and old, who, after being accused of helping the Security Battalions or as sympathizers on locals' testimonies, are then led to a location outside the village to be killed, their bodies being dumped in a well. According to tradition, EAM-ELAS fighters from other parts of Greece were used to carry out the killings, while Velouhiotis and the remaining local guerillas traveled back to Kalamata with roughly 60 seized senior leaders of the Security Battalions: When they reached Kalamata's main square, an enraged mob burst through the guerrilla ranks and lynched the remaining detainees, beating or stabbing a few of them to death or hanging them from the lamp posts in the plaza. At the well of Meligalas, hundreds of ex-combatants and local citizens were killed over the course of four days: The site sees the exhumation of 708 remains in 1945, although the current memorial lists 787 names from 61 communities, and other accounts place the death toll at 1144 or higher.

The Meligalas well

The collaborationists were Greeks, trained and supported by the Nazis to help them defeat the guerillas that killed many Germans and interfered with their main mission to conquer the world. During the NAZI occupation of Greece, ELAS forces started operating in 1942-1943 in Peloponisus, beginning to gain control over the area. The authorities involved in the German occupation formed Security Battalions to control them. These Security Battalions not only took part in anti-guerrilla operations but also aided in mass retaliation against the local civilian population. With the freedom of Greece nearing in 1944, ELAS began targeting the Security Battalions more and more.

Once the formation of the Security Battalions was announced, ELAS took a proactive approach and implemented a policy of terror to safeguard civilian loyalty; this was done chiefly in the Peloponnesus countryside close to the German quarters. The number of the Security Battalions increased with the communist position getting strengthened and both sides getting engaged in clashes. Blame for the Battle of Meligalas (the Meligalas Massacre) was put on ELAS later.

In September 1941, after the removal of German forces from Peloponisus, a fraction of the collaborationist forces in Kalamata pulled out, heading to Meligalas. A force of about 1,000 collaborationists was gathered there, but they were quickly surrounded by ELAS, about 1,200 detachments strong. After a grueling fight expanding over three days, the ELAS troops broke through the barricades and entered the town. The ELAS' victory brought about a massacre, leading to prisoners and civilians being executed near a well.

The Battle of Meligalas

The collaborationists placed a heavy machine gun in the clock tower of the Meligalas' main church, Agios Ilias, and dispersed 50 light machine guns they had in buildings around the church. On the morning of September 13, ELAS forces of 1,200 men started an offensive. The attack was carried out according to a strategy devised in collaboration with all the members.

ELAS also stationed its solitary 10.5-centimeter gun, commanded by artillery captain Kostas Kalogeropoulos, atop the Skala heights. The ELAS plan called for the 3/9 Battalion, led by Captain Tasos Anastasopoulos ("*Kolopilalas*"), to advance quickly from the outskirts of the settlement to the main square, allowing the Agios Ilias fort to be attacked from two sides.

A party of 30 partisans was assaulted at midday on September 14, tossing German teller mines on the barbed wire guarding Agios Ilias, but they were repulsed by the collaborationists in a hail of fire. The defenders' barriers were breached by a squad commanded by Basakidis, but without reinforcement, they were forced back into a counterattack led by Sergeant Major Panagiotis Benos. The sight of injured ELAS combatants, as well as word of a 'Battalionists' murder, increased the hostile attitude among civilians watching the conflict.

The leaders of the Security Battalions gathered in the council on the morning of September 15, but the council quickly halted when the house was hit by a mortar shell. Commander Major Papadopoulos recommended making an advance in the direction of Gargalianoi. However, the council was disbanded after a new ELAS offensive on Agios

Ilias, during which Basakidis' forces successfully pushed the Battalionists back with hand grenades and submachine rifles.

ELAS partisans fired light machine guns into the town's interior from their new positions while collaborationists began raising white flags in surrender. A small group of Battalionists led by Major Kazakos attempted to flee to the south and then to Derveni, but the Reserve ELAS, a squad of the 11th ELAS Regiment, and the Mavroskoufides confronted them on the heights near Anthousa and attacked, assassinating several. These events occurred over a period of four days. Hundreds of convicts were abruptly tried and executed as the guerrillas plundered and burned the village of Meligalas. About 1,144 or more people of both genders, regardless of their ages, were killed outside the village in a field. Their bodies were hurled down a nearby well. The number of people killed, however, is arguable, as there are 787 names on the crosses in a city. The number of casualties ranges between 700 and 1100 on different counts.

Following the spread of the massacre news, the ELAS leadership and the National Liberation Front (EAM) - their political parent group - took measures to warrant a peaceful transition of power in most parts of the country, off-putting retaliation.

Later in time, a chapel, an ossuary, a memorial wall, a field with hundreds of crosses displaying the names and ages of the dead, and a monument were erected by Greek Americans.

Reprisals and Executions

The end of the skirmish led civilians to invade Meligalas, resulting in unrestrained looting and massacre. As per a contemporary report found in the archives of the communist party of Greece (KKE), these were inhabitants of the Skala village that was set ablaze by the German Army.

Velouchiotis was among the captive battalionists held in Bedesten. Soon after the conclusion of the battle, he arrived at Meligalas with his private escort. There Velouchiotis recognized a gendarme who was earlier arrested and released and ordered his execution. The first wave of reprisal was implicitly encouraged by ELAS by purposely loose guarding its captives; this then caused a series of organized executions to ensue.

A bigoted court-martial prevailed in the town. This court immediately sentenced 60 officers and other leaders of the Battalions. A list of their names was also provided by local ELAS factions that included reasons for the actions taken against them, and those reasons had more to do with personal differences than crimes. The executions took place outside the town at an abandoned well.

To keep the executioners from being recognized, an ELAS detachment from a different squadron carried out the executions, probably a squadron of the 8th Regiment; the men in the squad belonged to Kosmas and Tsitalia in Arcadia.

On September 26, 1944, Major General Emmanouil Mantakas reported that "800 Rallides, the derogatory nickname for the Battalionists, after the collaborationist PM Ioannis Rallis were killed", a number repeated by Stefanos Sarafis in his own book on ELAS. A Red Cross report said that the number of people who were killed surpassed 1,000. However, a year later, the renowned Greek coroner Dimitrios Kapsaskis' team reported recovering 708 corpses from Meligalas.

Ilias Theodoropoulos' brother was also killed in Meligalas. In his book, Theodoropoulos states that 1,500 to 2,000 people were dead; he even provides a list containing the names of 1,144 people killed in action or executed by the ELAS, some of whom were lynched in Kalamata, including nine adolescents (one girl and nine boys), 18 elderly, and 22 women. Among those killed, 108 were from Meligalas.

The post-war right-wing establishment, however, claimed the tally to be much, with approximations ranging from 1,110 to more than 2,500 victims. Kosmas Antonopoulos, the National Radical Union politician whose father was also executed by ELAS, discussed in his writings that 2,100 people were executed at Meligalas but cites data for 699 people only. In contrast, authors sympathetic to ELAS reduce the number of executions considerably: the most detailed account calculates 120 killed in action, about 350 executed.

The ruling right-wing establishment eternalized the Meligalas Massacre as proof of communist brutality; it also memorialized the victims as devoted heroes. The official support of this commemoration stopped after the Metapolitefsi. The massacre is still honored by the progenies and sociopolitical sympathizers of the Security Battalions; it continues to be a point of reference for supporters to rally cry.

The Meligalas and Kalamata events proved to be damaging to ELAS, whose headship initially opposed the fact that a massacre had occurred. They were later coerced into acknowledging it and presenting a condemnation. Nevertheless, the more modest leaders of ELAS, Sarafis and Alexandros Svolos, contended that they devotedly acted upon the commands of the national unity government, issuing orders to "stop all executions." They showed the ELAS' willingness to suffer momentous losses to be able to regain control prior to the onset of British forces. ELAS' ability to succeed in this goal resulted in a shift in British policy.

The British liaison officers in Peloponisus, who until this point were told not to intervene in any events, were now commanded to get involved for safekeeping, securing the surrender, and delivering the weapons of Security Battalions to British forces to keep ELAS from the possession of those weapons.

Consequently, because of the arbitration of British liaisons, the Red Cross, the local ELAS powers, and the representatives of the Papandreou Government in many towns of Central Greece and Peloponnesus, Security Battalions gave in without bloodshed or combats. However, numerous Battalionists, having surrendered, were slain by civilian mobs or ELAS partisans, as at Pylos or in some places in northern Greece. This was the ultimate consequence of the prevalent desire for retaliation, but some cases also involved the assistance or even provocation of EAM cadres.

The social polarization between ELAS and its opponents, both liberal and nationalist anti-communists, resulted in the adoption of a sort of double talk. ELAS declared that it supported order and the restoration of government authority while at the same time launching a large-scale, illegal bloody eradication to be able to secure its political power before the influx of the British forces, better up its negotiating position within the government, and placate the popular demand for retaliation and esteem before the law. ELAS'S rivals, on the other hand, guaranteed its participation in the government while simultaneously trying to preserve the lives of the collaborationists.

On September 26, 1944, Papandreou, EDES leader Napoleon Zervas, Sarafis (on behalf of ELAS), and Scobie signed the Caserta

Agreement. The pact put ELAS and EDES under Scobie's command and titled the Security Battalions as "instruments of the enemy," ordering for them to be treated as hostile forces if they did not give in. After the signing of the agreement, Scobie's officers were ordered by him to intercede to guard the Battalionists, restricting them under guard.

In September 1944, communist guerrilla forces of EAM-ELAS encircled the retreating forces of the collaborationist Security Battalions. After overpowering them in tough combat, the guerrillas executed the militiamen who had surrendered, in addition to scores of civilians from the neighboring villages who allegedly sympathized with them.

A gigantic concrete cross that marks the site of the executions can still be seen today, in addition to the well where the bodies were thrown. This site is where a memorial wall, a field with hundreds of crosses with the names and ages of the martyred, monument, a chapel, and an ossuary are built to commemorate this massacre – the very massacre that marked the initial stages of the Greek Civil War. Decades have passed since, and the incident still divides politics and public opinion in Greece.

The Monastery of St. George Massacre

Feneos is a village and a former municipality in Corinthia, Peloponisus, Greece. It lies at the foot of Mount Cyllene, the mythical birthplace of God Hermes. Therefore, served as an important cult center for the god, particularly during the annual festival of the Hermes.

During the Greek Civil War, the communist Guerrillas turned the nearby monastery of St. George into a concentration camp and killing ground for those they deemed "reactionaries." The concentration camp was well-organized for mass killings, with six to seven resident killers that worked round the clock during busy times. It is believed that hundreds were killed.

The Monastery of Saint George, constructed close to the village of Kalivia Feneou in Corinthia, was one of the most notorious concentration camps. On March 1943, the ELAS followers killed the six monks and turned the monastery cellars into a prison different than other camps. Hostages did not stay there for long. After several days, they were taken to several nearby cliffs and another isolated site and were executed. A representative of the Peloponnesian Office of the ELAS, Vaggelis Zegos (nicknamed "*Stathes*" or "*Triantafyllos*"), supervised the executions.

The St George Monastery massacre

Zegos was also in charge of all operations against anti-communists and non-communists in Argolis, Corinthia, and northern

Arcadia to terrorize the countryside populations; he would arrest up to 10% of the inhabitants of each village for execution by ELAS, which lasted through June 1944.

When joint Greek and British troops (in 1944 December clashes in Athens) defeated ELAS, communist organizations were disarmed (thousands of firearms were kept concealed, though, and utilized in the "third round" of the war in 1946-1949) and the novel National Guard reinstated government control in most of the countryside areas, including Feneos.

Rumors were spread by locals, and right-wing newspapers claimed that ELAS had arrested and executed 5,000 to 7,000 or even 13,000 people. However, bodies that were found in the area amounted to less than 4,000, out of which only 1,800 could be recognized. The government erected a monument for them with the names of the recognized victims inscribed on the walls of the structure. Ceremonies in memory were held every year, but they stopped as part of the reconciliation policy promoted by the PASOK socialist government after 1981.

The crimes and executions committed by the KKE during the Civil War were too many to mention in this book, but the most serious crime committed against the Greek people was the deportation of more than 30,000 Greek children to neighboring communist countries to be turned into communists and trained to fight their own country conducted by their new communist countries like Albania, Bulgarians, and others in the communist bloc. The Greek Civil War was among the most destructive, divisive, bitter civil wars that had a long-lasting effect on the lives of the Greek people that is felt to this day and will remain a stain in the Greek history books.

Chapter 11:
My Trip to Vambakou

One bright summer morning, my brother Argiri asked me to "Get ready. We are going to Vambakou." I didn't ask why because I knew the answer and I was ready and happy to go.

Vambakou was the name of the village where my aunt Theodora lived with her husband, Panagioti. It would be my second time visiting them. The first time was over three years ago during summer when I was much younger and spent more than two months with them. I had made a few new friends there and hoped to meet them again. We had a lot of fun together.

This time, I was much older. "It would only be for two or three weeks, or maybe until Mother delivered the new baby," my brother told me.

Babies in the village are usually delivered by a midwife or a *MAMI* in the expectant mother's home, and they didn't want kids in the way, deterring them from the difficult task at hand. I didn't understand their reasoning, but I was more than happy to go, so I could play with my old friends. I was looking forward to seeing them again.

My brother helped me up on Truman's *samari* (saddle), but the *samari* was much more than a saddle. It was made from maple wood with a smooth padded liner to fit snuggly and comfortably on the mule's back. It had metal hooks to hang everything from farming tools to *sakoulia* (homemade bags with a handle) to hang and carry firewood, sacks of potatoes, or any other commodity. It was sturdy enough to even give rides to young kids like me or old folks who could not walk. The samari was tightly strapped around Truman's belly with a leather strap, but even the strap sometimes couldn't prevent it from falling under his belly if the load was unbalanced.

Aunt Theodora's village was a two-hour walk away through hills and thick forests, with a stretch of a dangerously narrow road built at the side of a tall mountain. The road overlooked a deep canyon, where a single misstep of a mule or human would result in a tumble down to the bottom of the 200-foot canyon. I asked my brother, "Do you know about any accidents that occurred in the past.?"

He reluctantly answered, "Yes, there was only one."

Naturally, I asked my brother to narrate it to me, and he began. "Aunt Theodora's mule was loaded with two large sacs full of chestnuts; it stumbled on the way and lost its balance, falling over to the bottom of the canyon with the two sacs full of freshly picked chestnuts scattered all through the way leading to the bottom."

This was not good to hear, especially when we were about to cross the dangerous road. To my relief, my brother said, "They now have widened the road a bit to avoid such accidents. It's safe unless the road is washed away by heavy rains."

We started on our way to Vambakou, my brother walking ahead of Truman. He held a guide rope tied to Truman's *kapistrada* (a leader harness around the mule's head) to ensure he followed him and did not wander around looking for a green spot of grass to graze on.

It was a beautiful mid-summer morning. I could see the peaks of the mountains ahead and the bright orange rays—the color of hope, I would say—bursting out from behind the mountain peak like a ball of fire, slowly spreading a golden blanket and covering the entire landscape.

Truman trotted and shook me around like a leaf on a tree. I could hear birds singing, dogs barking, and cowbells ringing as the cows grazed around. I was lost, enjoying the view, when suddenly, a herd of goats appeared, their bells rattling like Santa's reindeer. They were running across the road, forcing us to stop until all of them—about a hundred goats and sheep with their young—crossed, leaving a massive cloud of dust behind them.

Soon after this unexpected delay, we continued to our destination of Vambakou while trying to clear the dust off our eyes and faces. My brother kept looking back to ensure I was not falling asleep because he knew from experience how easy it was for a kid to fall asleep while riding a mule, trotting through the narrow, winding paths full of rocks.

Suddenly, a loud machine-gun fire broke out a few hundred yards from us. Bullets were whizzing all around us with mortar shells and hand granades exploding with sharp objects flying over our heads. My brother helped me down from the mule and grabbed my hand. "Stop crying and run for cover as fast as you can," my brother said. We found a large boulder close by and hid behind it.

The battle raged for over an hour while we tried to stay calm and quiet, hoping it would end soon. We had no idea who was fighting. "It must be the Andartes fighting with the Greek soldiers, but I am unsure," my brother said.

After a while, a Greek soldier, with his rifle ready, came running and saw us crouched down behind the boulder. He stopped, pointed his rifle at us, and asked, "Who are you? Are you with the Andartes?"

My brother explained to him how we got there and where we were going.

He moved his rifle away, saying, "Do not move till the battle is over. We ran into a band of Andartes and killed several of them. It seems that the rest of them have run into the forest. We are on the lookout for them."

Just before he was ready to join his group in the battle, I let out a painful scream because of a sharp pain coming from my right leg.

The soldier knew a bullet had hit me; he instantly put down his rifle, took out some bandages from his service pack, and wrapped it tightly around my bleeding leg. Then he took out a small plastic package and gave me a capsule to take, saying, "Take this to relieve the pain." Then, he turned to my brother. "He is lucky the bullet didn't break any bones. It's just a tiny flesh wound, so he should be OK to get where you are going," the soldier added. He then picked up his rifle and ran up the hill. We never saw him again.

The battle seemed to have ended shortly after because the machine gun rattle stopped. My brother stood up and looked around. "All is quiet," he said. "How do you feel about continuing the trip? Are you ready to move on, or should we return home?

The capsule the soldier gave me seemed to have done its job. The pain had subsided for the time being, so I said to him, "We should continue our trip if you think it is safe because the Andartes would want to take revenge on us after the battle."

He took a few minutes to think about our situation and then decided it was safe for us to continue our trip. He said, "The Antartes must be busy attending to their wounded. We should take a chance and move on." I knew his mission was to take me away for a couple of weeks while our mother was delivering a baby with the help of the midwife (*MAMI*) back home. I knew I was not supposed to be around.

My brother said to me, "Sit up and see if you can walk." I did, and the pain came back when I stepped on my foot, but I could tolerate it. My brother helped me up on Truman, and we resumed our trip.

We were now about to enter the beautiful green forest, and I was dying to get down and walk around, but I knew I could not do that now. So, I enjoyed the magical beauty while riding Truman. I just enjoyed the beauty of the forest and momentarily took the pain away. The ground was covered with fallen brown leaves, twigs, pine needles, pinecones, and small branches. I thought about the myriad of inhabitants who lived in the forest and thrived harmoniously inside their silent kingdom.

There were fallen trees that looked like fallen soldiers in a battle, and the sight and smell of resin flowing out of the pine trees, colorful berry bushes, and thick underbrush. I heard birds singing and saw them hopping from one branch to another, sometimes even moving from tree to tree. There were bees buzzing and hurrying from flower to flower, collecting nectar to carry back to their beehives. The squirrels chattered, and lizards rummaged through tree bark. I could hear trickling water running nearby and saw a small rabbit jump out of his hiding place, hopping away from harm's way. There was a turtle with its head out of its shell, slowly walking in circles, and then there were insects creeping and butterflies floating all around me.

I smelled the earthy smell of the forest, wildflowers, animal scents, rotting wood, scents on the wind from nearby places, water, wood smoke (bogs, stagnant pools of water, dead animals), skunks, and skunk weed. Riding through the narrow winding roads, the forest reminded me of my village-- dogs barking, birds flying and singing all around me, and the loud sounds of donkeys and other animals in mating seasons.

My brother said, "We are about to leave the forest, and soon, we will be entering the dangerous stretch of the road that I told you about. When we get there, you must come off Truman for safety reasons. If Truman stumbles, and mules often do, you could fall off the cliff and into the deep canyon." He then reminded me of the road again, saying, "This is the most dangerous part of our trip, a narrow, jagged section of the road that runs at the edge of a tall mountain." The road was now in our view. From my vantage point, it looked like a white line running across the middle of a tall mountain until it disappeared, getting wrapped around the mountain. It surely was not a road for the faint of heart.

I was so disappointed that we had to leave the beautiful forest. I turned to look around one last time and say goodbye to all of God's gifts to humanity. I saw a tall deer standing on top of a rock with its beautiful antlers and big eyes wide open, its big ears looking like radar watching us leaving its kingdom.

I wanted to say goodbye, so I freed my right hand from holding on to the samari and waved at this beautiful forest animal that stood like a soldier guarding his kingdom. As we reached the dangerous road, my brother stopped and, careful not to move my injured leg, helped me down from Truman. He asked me again, "How does your leg feel?"

I said, "It is starting to hurt me more now."

"Probably the medicine the soldier gave you is wearing you down," he replied.

My brother held me while I walked to minimize the pressure on my injured leg. We walked very slowly and carefully on this narrow road with Truman trotting behind us. We came to a section where the road was cut off and stopped. My brother said, "This is the result of a rainstorm that washed about three feet of the road away." He blinked, then added, "I was afraid we might run into a problem like this, but not of such a magnitude; it often happens in this area."

We stood there for a few minutes, pondering. "Since you can't jump yourself..." He stooped down and gestured to me to get on his back. I wrapped both of my hands around his neck. "Hold tight," he warned. He wanted to be sure I didn't fall off when he jumped. "Do not look down; close your eyes," he said, continuing with his warnings. I was frightened for myself, my brother, and even Truman as to how'd we cross this road break. It would be terrible for our entire family if we lost Truman; he gave us our lives back by helping to cultivate the farms and eliminate starvation.

I could hear my heart beating like a drum. "One...two...three..." My brother counted and jumped. I closed my eyes, panting upon feeling death so up close. He landed on his belly with me on top of him, but we were both safe on the other side. We both let out a big sigh and did our cross, happy that we had made it. Now it was Truman's turn.

We were looking back at Truman standing on the edge of the break, waiting for our signal. My brother was more confident than I that Truman would make it. He knew very well that all animals could sense danger and are determined to survive, especially mules, who have a special sense of survival. We gave Truman a few seconds to concentrate on his jump. Then my brother pulled the rope and yelled, "*ELA!*" (come). Truman trotted closer to the open road, stopped for a few seconds, then took a giant leap like a deer and landed safely on our side.

We both sighed in relief, knowing we had evaded a potentially disastrous outcome. "I knew he would do it," my brother enthusiastically said and patted him on his behind. I hugged Truman's long face and gave him a big kiss.

"My brother was right; you could do it," I said. If he could have talked, he would have said, "Thank you, my friends."

Crossing this dangerous part of the road, we left behind the beautiful forest, entering a different type of forest now. There was an array of trees instead of tall pines as in the previous forest. These trees, with their rounded tops, looked like huge open umbrellas. There were hundreds of them stretching out as far as we could see. My brother said, "These are all chestnut trees where the chestnuts you like so much come from."

My brother said, "This literally is a chestnut country, rich in chestnuts that are supplied throughout the country and around the world."

Once again, I wanted to get down and walk around to see another gift of God that this forest was. I could not, of course; the pain now was intolerable. "Hurry up and get us to Aunt Theodora's as soon as possible," I said to my brother.

144

My brother nodded and said, "We will get more medicine to help with the pain. We should be there in 20 minutes." He then pulled the rope, telling Truman to move faster.

When we arrived, Aunt and Uncle were waiting for us at their house's entrance. They were very excited to see us, but my leg wrapped with bandages worried my aunt. Blood had seeped through the bandage, making for an uncanny view. Frantically, she asked, "What happened to your leg?"

My brother told them the entire story.

"You should directly go to see the village doctor. Go right away!" my aunt insisted, almost crying.

We hoped the doctor was in the village because he served all the villages in the area for two days a week each. My aunt remembered that day was one of the two days the doctor would be in his office in their village.

"Follow me on the way to the doctor's office; it's just two blocks away," my aunt said.

Luckily, the doctor was in when we reached. I was helped down from Truman and up a few steps into the doctor's office. The pain was unbearable by now, and I was beginning to tear up.

The doctor removed the bandages, looked at the wound, and shook his head. "The bullet just missed the tabula," he said.

"What is tabula?" I asked.

"The bone," the doctor replied. "This is an open flesh wound, and if it didn't receive proper treatment on time, infection could have set in."

First, the doctor gave me a shot, then cleaned the wound with an antiseptic swab and applied some ointment. He went on to stitch the open wound, which is when I realized the shot was given to make me numb to the pain of stitches; the stitches didn't hurt at all. When the doctor was done stitching up my wound, he rebandaged the wound with clean and proper bandages. "Bring me back next week when I am in the office," he told my brother.

My aunt and brother brought me back to my aunt's house, where she had dinner ready for us. We had my favorite fruits—roasted *castañas* chestnuts and grapes—for dessert. It was late in the evening when we finished dinner, and the sun was still up. My brother had to get back home that very night. They tried to change his mind and lure him into leaving in the morning.

"If I leave now, I will be home before sundown," my brother said, gearing to leave. "You please behave and listen to Aunt and Uncle. I will come back to pick you up in two or three weeks," he added. He hugged and kissed all of us and left with Truman. Seeing him off, I reminded him, "Careful on the dangerous road. Take care!"

Chapter 12:
The Fate of the Greek Children

A Greek Tragedy During the Geek Civil War

The Greek communist Party, KKE, kidnapped and deported over 30,000 Greek children to Albania and other communist countries. They raided their homes and took children by force from their families, sending them to Albania and other communist countries to be turned into communists. They trained them to go back to fight their own brothers and fathers when the civil war was over to live in a communist Greece if the guerillas won the civil war.

Queen Frederica had established a Royal Fund to build children's villages all over the country to guard against communist kidnappings in conflict zones. More than 20,000 children were taken into care and returned to their families following the end of World War II in 1950. Although most of the parents were Guerilla communists, the Communist Party KKE used the argument that the children were sent to communist countries with their parent's approval.

Institutions for Children

Children in communist countries were housed in specially constructed children's homes. Under the name "Committee for the Aid of

147

the Child," these orphanages were jointly run by the Greek Communist Party and the government of the host country. Most of them ended up becoming citizens of the communist countries they were raised in. A law allowing the return of all Greek-national children was passed in 1982. Only a small percentage of the children evacuated from Greece were of Slavic or Macedonian origin.

"Children's homes" in each of the host countries operated under the same rules. These institutions were all-inclusive and isolated from the rest of the world; they went about their daily activities in complete quarantine. Greece's Communist Party insisted that the houses' operations be kept secret and not mixed in with the public. Not even the children's parents were allowed to communicate with their own children. All correspondence between their parents was rigorously edited.

A group of women refugees from Northern Greece who had accompanied the retreating guerillas into Albania seized the opportunity to help the kidnapped children cope with their new life in a new country and presented themselves as their mothers. Most children saw them as their own mothers, and they developed a deep affection for them. The name of the group given to the children was called "Adelphi" (brothers).

Their Daily Training Regiments

Their daily routine was commanded by a strict program. The discussions were solely dedicated to obedience and strict discipline. In some cases, physical punishment was used as a form of discipline in most communist countries. The students were taught the host country as well as the Greek language and communist ideals by good communist teachers.

The powerful KKE believed that these children they would return to Greece as adults and free the country from the oppressive regime.

The indoctrination of the teenagers at a community of children's homes near Dresden was unusually intense, as they were preparing to liberate their motherland, Greece, from the fascist regime and went through military training. After they learned the language of the host country, the teenagers were sent to technical schools that were not their first choice and then placed in industrial jobs. In the meantime, the Greek Communist Party in Greece began to lose power.

The Psychological Effects on These Captive Children

Many studies were made to examine the immediate or long-term psychological impacts had on the children who were removed from their homes and families and transported to communist countries. These children were likely affected by a series of negative life experiences, including war conditions in their villages and the extreme violence of the civil war.

The family breakdown and the breakup of family ties, the dangerous and long journey out of their country, and all the years spent in total institutions called (children's homes) had a huge impact on these children. But there has been no research done on the immediate and long-term health effects of these children being removed from their parent's homes and putting them in children's homes in communist countries (total institutions).

The loss of childhood has finally been recognized by adults, wondering who's going to bring back their childhood. When they were reunited with their parents, the now-adult children were cold and detached.

Having grown up in a different country under communist norms, most parents could not rejoin their children. The Greek Government refused to allow some of the young people to return to their country and were relocated to the western world.

The Aegean Macedonian refugees formed an international network in support of their right to return to their homes. It was the greatest fear of all Greek mothers to have their son or daughter taken away and forced to live alone in a communist system of children's homes. If they had to choose, even death would be preferable to living the way they did. To die in their native land, some former children of Eastern bloc countries have returned to Greece in their senior years.

It was not uncommon for people to send their young children, grandchildren, and even nephews to Greece to be raised by a Greek family.

Most of Yugoslavia's post-World War II refugees came from the Socialist Republic of Macedonia because the borders were so close, and many ethnic Macedonians from Yugoslavia entered Greece trying to help the Guerillas win the civil war.

Before the border with Yugoslavia was closed, thousands more refugees, partisans, and exiles joined them, forcing all the kidnapped children to enter Yugoslavia. There were many abandoned villages and places in Macedonia where the Greek Macedonian refugees settled after fleeing Greece.

Most of the newcomers settled in the towns of Tetovo and Gostivar. Bitola and the surrounding area were to be the new home for another large group of refugees, with camps in Kumanovo and Strumica.

Some of the largest concentrations of refugees and their descendants can be found in the Skopje suburbs of Avtokomanda and Topansko Pole.

Many of them were well-educated and integrated into Macedonian society, and most of them never returned to Greece after their exodus. Greek refugees fleeing the civil war fled to Macedonia in large numbers. More than 50,000 refugees and their descendants are believed to be living there.

Most Macedonians, Greek, and Aromanian Macedo-Romanian children were evicted from communist-controlled territories. As a result of their predicament, they have been dubbed "the refugee children." About 28,000 to 32,000 children were thought to have been rescued in the years between 1948 and 1949. Vojvodina became home to one of the largest refugee populations in the Eastern Bloc, even though many children were ethnic Macedonians who spoke Macedonian as their first language.

Refugees were housed in the ex-German camp of Buljkes in Yugoslavia. The so-called "Greek Commune" was formed by most of the refugees who were members of the K.K.E.-ELAS, which was a political party. Even though many of the "Greeks" were Slav Macedonians, it is known that many of the "Greeks" were actual Greeks. In the spring of 1946, a group of Greek Macedonian refugees, approximately 250 people, left the camp. Wherever the evacuees ended up in the Eastern bloc, there were special provisions in place for them. Ethnic Macedonian refugees were given the opportunity to learn both their native language and the language of their new host country, with many opting to study Russian as well.

After the collapse of the Greek communist army, thousands of partisans were sent to Tashkent and Alma Ata in Central Asia. The Soviet Union received an estimated 11,980 Partisans, 8,573 of whom were men and 3,407 of whom were women. Ethnic Macedonian and Greek partisans were separated during the 1960s and 1970s, with many Greek partisans remaining in the Soviet Union. After the amnesty law of 1980, many Greeks returned to Greece, particularly to Greek Macedonia.

The Refugee Exodus

Albania had been part of the eastern communist bloc and was collaborating and helping the Andartes (guerillas) to eventually defeat the Greek army and deliver Greece to the Russians—a long-sought strategic plan to gain control and bring it into the Communist bloc.

After the civil war ended, thousands of the kidnapped Greek children were allowed to return to their country. However, many stayed in Albania after their rigid indoctrination into the communist system and trained to fight against their own country, Greece. I will talk more about the kidnapped children in the later chapters.

Poland

More than 12,300 refugees have entered the Lower Silesia region of Poland since the beginning of 2015. This group included both Greeks and Macedonians, both of whom were ethnic Macedonians. Some of the Greek refugee children who had been sent to Romania ended up at Ldek-Zdrój in Kroscienko, where a new camp had been established, on October 25. Poland's Red Cross-aided facilities were well-staffed and technologically advanced. Refugee camps were set up in Gdansk and Zgorzelec for those who remained in Lower Silesia, while most of them were spread across southern and central Poland. Many Greeks returned to Greece following the Amnesty Law of 1982, while a significant number of Slav Macedonians left Poland for the Socialist Republic of Macedonia.

Czechoslovakia

Once in Czechoslovakia, refugee children were put into an old German camp for quarantine and bathing. Refugee children were fed and housed as they were sorted into age groups in this facility. The younger children were taken care of by surrogate mothers from Greek Macedonia, while the older children were sent to school.

The children were well-trained by the Czech teachers who had received psychology training. They were taught Czech, Greek, Macedonian, and Russian in Czechoslovakia. The Greek children had to be relocated because of their conflict with ethnic Macedonian children. Older Partisans and ex-communists eventually joined the children.

Approximately 4,000 men, 3,475 women, and 4,148 children were evacuated to Czechoslovakia by 1950, according to official estimates. Greece and Macedonia each had their own neighborhoods by 1960. While most refugees fled to other communist countries, most chose to remain in Czechoslovakia. In the 1980s, many Greeks returned to their homeland. In the early 1990s, the Czech Republic and Slovakia established branches of the Association of Refugee Children from the Aegean Part of Macedonia.

Czech teachers with psychology training did their best to educate the students. In Czechoslovakia, they learned Czech, Greek, Macedonian, and Russian. Children of Greek descent had to be separated from their ethnic Macedonian peers due to growing hostilities. Senior Partisans and ex-communists eventually joined the children.

Unlike in other communist countries, most refugees chose to remain in Czechoslovakia. During the 1980s, a significant number of Greeks returned to their homeland. Czech and Slovak branches of a Macedonia-based children's refugee organization were established early in the 1990s. The government of the Czech Republic later recognized the Greek refugees as a national minority.

Bulgaria

The People's Republic of Bulgaria initially refused to accept many refugees from Macedonia, but later, the policy changed, and the Bulgarian government actively sought ethnic Macedonian refugees. A total of 2,500 children and 3,000 partisans fled to Bulgaria in the final months of the conflict. Higher numbers of refugees arrived in 1944 when the Bulgarian Army withdrew from the Drama-Serres region. Macedonians have a large immigrant population in the United States.

Eastern Bloc refugees were enticed to relocate to Sofia (Bulgaria) by the "Slavic Committee." A political study from 1962 found that 6,529 Greeks had made the journey to the United States to pursue careers in politics. As in other Eastern Bloc countries, there were no special institutions set up to deal with the unique challenges faced by child refugees.

This has led to an increase in membership in the "Association of Refugee Children from the Aegis of Macedonia," a Macedonian non-governmental organization. These migrants were quickly integrated into Bulgarian society after they fled to the Republic of Macedonia.

Romania

A massive evacuation camp was set up in Tulgheş, Romania. More than one hundred small kids and babies were reunited with their guardians at this site. Around 5,132 children, 1,981 men, and 1,939 women were evacuated to Romania, according to official estimates at the time. Romania received the vast majority of the Eastern Bloc's evacuees. Special arrangements had been made for the children. They also learned Russian, Greek, and Macedonian in addition to Romanian during their time in Romania. Slav-Macedonian refugee children were officially recognized as a minority community following the passage of the Amnesty Law in 1982.

Hungary

Many refugees were also relocated to Hungary between 1946 and 1949. There were 2,161 males, 2,233 females, and 2,859 minors in the total population of the city. The first 2,000 children were taken to Hungary, where they were held in military camps for the duration of the war. Buljkes also sent a second party to Hungary, this time consisting of 1,200 partisans.

It wasn't long before a refugee camp was established in the village of Fehervarcsurgo in Hungary. According to their village of origin, the groups were quickly divided up by the authorities. After that, they were "adopted" by the Hungarian community. Nikos Beloyannis, a Greek communist fighter, was the inspiration for the town's Greek name, Beloiannisz, in central Hungary. While scattered across the country, they received assistance and education from the Red Cross.

Thousands of Hungarians emigrated in search of family and friends. Ethnic Greeks fled to the Socialist Republic of Macedonia or returned to Greece after the fall of the communist regime in Greece in 1982.

The German People's Republic

During World War II, East Germany received an estimated 1,200 child refugees. They were all referred to as "Greek" at the time because there was no distinction between their ethnicities. Besides the Macedonian and Albanian children, there were also a few other children. Macedonian was not taught in Germany, unlike the rest of Eastern Europe, due to most Macedonians being Greek. Most Greek children would return to their home country after finishing their education in the United States.

Many people fled Greece even after the civil war ended because of the widespread destruction caused by the civil war, particularly in Macedonia and Epirus. As a result of their ties to the Bulgarians, some people were expelled from the country by government forces. Tens of thousands of people fled across the border before the Greek government was able to regain control of the former Communist-controlled area.

Over a million people were forced from their homes in Russia's former Soviet Union. Many ended up in Eastern Bloc countries like the Soviet Union and Czechoslovakia, while others ended up in countries like Australia, the United States, and Canada. As a result of this process, many families were shattered, with brothers and sisters being separated from each other. In many cases, mothers had no further contact with their children and had no idea where they were.

Adults were fleeing Europe in large numbers and making their way to the United States, Canada, and Australia. Thousands of people would later move to the United States, and more than 2,000 refugee children came to Canada alone in the 1950s. Cities like London and Paris were overflowing with migrants.

The social and political climate of Greek Macedonia was profoundly altered by the exodus of a significant portion of the population. Following the Greek Civil War, issues of depopulation, repatriation, discrimination, and repopulation would arise.

Citizenship Can Be Revoked

Anyone who had been critical of the government or had fled Greece was stripped of their citizenship in 1947. In many cases, they were denied the opportunity of returning to Greece, either permanently or temporarily. Exiles and refugees were unable to return to their homeland because of this.

There were many Eastern Europeans who chose to stay in Eastern Europe or flee to Western Europe. Exiles' citizenship was taken away without an independent tribunal or other internationally recognized standards for citizenship seizure, such as legal representation and the right to self-defense, being granted to them.

According to the report, this mechanism of citizenship seizure had "historically been employed against those identifying as ethnic Macedonians. Every American, regardless of race or ethnicity, must comply with it. It has only been applied to citizens who identify as belonging to the "Macedonian minority" except in one case.

It is possible for dual citizens with Greek citizenship to be denied entry to Greece using their second nationality's passport, as stated in Article 20 of the Citizenship Code. A law of amnesty was enacted by the Greek Government in 1982. Law 400/76 allowed Greek political exiles

157

who had fled the country during the Greek Civil War to return and repatriate. According to a ministerial edict, only "all Greeks by genus who left abroad as political refugees during the Civil War of 1946–1949" could return to the country. Bulgars and ethnic Macedonians, who weren't "Greeks by genus," were also excluded.

It was the most devastating, painful, and never forgotten war crime to the Greek population, especially to those parents who witnessed their children being forcefully dragged away and never to see them again. Some returned many years later but could no longer accept them as their children because their ideology and, in most cases, their religious beliefs were no longer the same as before they were kidnapped. This cruel kidnapping and drafting of children into military service came to be known as the "Paidomazoma."

Chapter 13:
The Elona Story

Kids are naïve, but their naivety can sometimes make them do seriously risky, stupid, and even life-threatening things. In this chapter, you will find one such journey that two young boys took in the war-ravaged areas.

This is a story about two young boys who risked their lives as they walked over 40 miles to reach a monastery named Elona. Their intention was pure; they wanted to visit Elona to pray for their families, especially for riddance from the civil war after over three years of suffering under the Nazi occupation.

Fear, sadness, anxiety, and helplessness were the four major emotions we experienced. We were always on the lookout for something bold and cheerful to pass our time and to replace our constant hopelessness and despair. We were tired of watching our parents struggle to feed and clothe us and keep us alive, constantly trying to keep us from hunger and sickness during the ongoing wars for over seven years. Now we lived in a village where brothers were killing brothers, and you couldn't trust your friends or neighbors any longer.

My friends and I were anxious, hopeless, and fearful of being kidnapped and shipped to communist Albania to grow up in a communist system and return to kill the Greeks that may have survived the civil war. To avoid such a tragedy, our parents did not allow us to roam around the village streets alone, which added to our hopelessness and despair.

Albania had been part of the eastern communist bloc and was collaborating and helping the Andartes (guerillas) to eventually defeat the Greek army and deliver Greece to the Russians—a long-sought strategic plan to gain control and bring it into the Communist bloc.

After the civil war ended, thousands of the kidnapped Greek children were allowed to return to their country. However, many stayed in Albania after their rigid indoctrination into the communist system and trained to fight against their own country, Greece. I will talk more about the kidnapped children in the later chapters.

One miserable rainy day, all four of us were sitting underneath the house stairs at Taki's, wondering what we could do to change our lives without getting killed or kidnapped. We felt lost and were very desperate to find a solution or a way we could help ourselves.

One exclaimed, "We can go to church and pray."

Then Bill jumped in and said, "My mother is planning to go to Elona Monastery to pray for the civil war to end and save her family. Her mother took her there when she was a child riding a donkey, and she is going to visit it again now."

Nobody seemed excited about going to a monastery when nobody knew where this monastery was and how we would get there.

I thought it was a thrilling idea and asked Bill to find out more information about this monastery from his mother, like the location, how long it would take us to get there, and the fastest route to get there if she knew. After we had all the information needed, we would discuss the potential risks and decide if the trip was worth taking. Bill agreed and told us he would talk to his mother and get back to us soon.

Our "highly classified meeting" suddenly ended when Taki's mother called us in for lunch. We all ran up the stairs and sat at the kitchen table. Taki's mother had some leftover baked chicken with potatoes—our favorite meal—with bread and freshly made Greek cheese from their herd of goats his father had.

We enjoyed our lunch while we kept looking at each other like a bunch of spies planning a covert operation, with suspicious looks on our faces.

Taki's mother commented, "Why do you all look kind of serious today?" She wondered if we had done something wrong.

Taki said, "No, Mom, we are just tired."

We all thanked her for the delicious lunch and headed home. On the way home, we agreed to meet the next day to continue our plan, and I asked everyone to bring some new ideas.

A few days later, Bill walked over to my house to fill me in on what his mother had told him about the monastery. "She said she had been to Elona as a child with her mother, riding a donkey. She knows all about this well-known monastery for its miracles; this was the place where many sick people went to get well," Bill said, then paused. "It is a very long and dangerous walking trip for young kids like yourselves, especially now with a civil war," she added.

It took Taki's and Bill's mothers over 12 hours to get there, both riding a slow but steady donkey with several stops on the way. They were able to carry more food, water, and other items as they had a donkey to ride on. We, however, planned to be walking all the way.

Upon asking more about the journey, Bill told me, "She also mentioned many other horror stories during the occupation and the current civil war: women getting raped, young kids kidnapped, and many other frightening stories." That should have made us all change our minds about such a dangerous trip.

Taki asked, "Why go to Elona to pray? We are not sick; we can go to our church here in our village to pray and don't have to travel the long and dangerous distance to pray." It was indeed a very logical question for us to ponder and answer ourselves before we decided to go to Elona.

Bill's mother's story was an intriguing one but almost unbelievable. Two women taking such a long and dangerous trip riding a donkey during the summer heat seemed to be a little far-fetched account. Bill and I looked each other in the eyes with a wondrous look, both touched by his mother and grandmother's courage in taking that long trip, knowing very well the potential risks.

We had a few minutes to ponder Bill's mother's words and felt slightly discouraged. We needed to discuss the new information with the others, so we walked over to Taki's house, where they both were waiting for us to hear what Bill's mother had to say. Bill and I knew they would reject our plan; they had gotten cold feet before this new information from Bill's mother.

If that was not a deterring message from Bill's mother not to even think of such a trip, it was a warning of the dangers we may have to face. For some, it could be considered a stern warning to stay home, but to Bill and me, two young and robust kids, it seemed like a great adventure, and the possibility of going was still alive and well. We were excited.

Bill's mother had him almost convinced to go to Elona, but not alone. She told him, "You can go but with at least one of your friends to pray for your families and all the Greek people suffering under Nazi occupation and now a civil war." She even showed him how to get there using an old map that her mother used when they went to Elona many years ago.

Bill and I had a private conversation without Taki and Themis, as we knew they would not go with us. Both of us agreed to take the journey. The only detail left for me was to ask my mother if I could go with my cousin Bill without the others, as they saw it as too dangerous and not a fun trip.

When I approached my mother with our bold plans, she opposed the idea of us walking that long through dangerous mountains, especially with the Andartes around looking for kids like us to kidnap and send to Albania. After she pondered for a few minutes, she told me, "Let me talk to Bill's mother, and I will let you know."

A few days later, they met, and because (luckily) both of them believed in miracles and knew a lot about those that had taken place before, they agreed to let us go after thorough preparation of things we needed to carry with us. My mother said, "Start with making a detailed list of all the items you need to take and keep a special focus on the two essentials: food and water."

Very excited, Bill and I were getting all the items on the list ready, except food, of course, because we had to wait for that, and we wanted no delay to embark on our journey. The mere thought of walking to Elona, 55kl, roughly 40 miles each way, should have made us change our plans for something less adventurous, or at least postpone this plan till we got a bit older and the country was free from wars and fear of being killed or kidnapped. But none of it did; nothing made us change our plans.

We started getting all the items we needed to carry; our list included the following:

1. Food
2. Water
3. A blanket
4. A flashlight
5. A small kerosine lamp with enough kerosine to last at least one full night.
6. A pair of clean pants and a shirt for church
7. Miscellaneous items, like a pocket knife, first aid kit, etc.

Our friends and many adults couldn't believe Bill and I were planning such a dangerous trip. Only adults with experience could be walking through thick, hazardous forests and facing myriads of real dangers involving the Andartes, Hites (a right-wing faction fighting the communist andartes), and wild animals well known for their fierce attacks on people.

One of the most significant threats to our survival was falling and sustaining injuries needing medical attention, which would not be available unless it happened close to the monastery. That was a significant concern for all, including us, but it was not a deterrent factor, and the green light stayed on.

To this day, I don't know where such courage and commitment came from. I asked my mother later in my life, and she said, "It was a divine calling." Maybe it was! My mother was a big believer in religious miracles.

We planned to leave the following weekend and started going through the list. Our mothers were preparing our *sakoulia* sacs like a backpack filled with all the items listed above.

We needed a good pair of shoes to last us both ways. Luckily, I had a good brand-new pair of boots Uncle Gus had sent me from America; it seemed like I was saving them for this long hike to Elona. My mother told me, "Do not let anybody take them away, especially the Andartes. Next to food, shoes, especially boots, are the most frequent items seized by the Andartes."

Finally, after gathering all the items on our list, we were ready to depart. Bill was supposed to come to my house, and we would leave no later than 4 a.m. to embark on the journey. We chose the wee hours because it was mid-summer, which made it even more challenging to walk under the scorching sun during the day. To limit the challenges that we were enlisting for ourselves, we had to leave early morning. At that moment, I was reminded of the time I used to get up to go hunting or set the "angistria" hooks to catch big birds and bring them home for my mother to cook dinner.

Getting up early in the village was always worth it. You could smell the flowers, breathe the fresh air, listen to the birds, the roosters singing, and the dogs barking. It was like listening to an orchestra celebrating life and nature, but I was not going to a concert; I was going to a holy place to pray for our lives and the freedom that was snatched from us, first by the Nazis and now by the Andartes.

The most anticipated and yearned-for morning arrived, and Bill knocked on our door. When I opened it, he was standing there with a big smile on his face. He gestured with his hand and said, "Let's go, Giorgo." My mother was standing behind me doing her cross. Then she hugged and kissed us both and wished us a good and safe trip on our long walk to Elona to pray for all of us.

We followed the road shown on the map Bill's mother gave us and walked through the village to the outskirts, then onto a narrow winding road full of small and a few large rocks, being careful not to slip and fall as we kept walking and talking among ourselves mostly about our families.

About an hour into our trip, suddenly, a rabbit jumped out of his hiding bush in front of us, running for his life. I said to Bill, "He is lucky I don't have my father's shotgun with me. He wouldn't be running too far." Bill was not a hunter and made no comments.

We continued walking through the thick forest, up and down hills, hiking for a couple of hours without any incidents. We reached the top of a steep hill and looked down on the other side; we both got a bit scared by the steep slope. We were afraid we might slip and roll to the bottom, almost 100 ft. straight down.

"That's scary," Bill said.

"It is," I agreed and added, "but we can't go back. There must be a way out. Let's try to find it."

We looked to see if there was another way to go around this steep slope and prevent any possible accident, but all options seemed worse than to start stepping instead of walking down the hill.

Finding no other way, Bill said, "Oh, boy! What are we going to do now?"

"We advance. What else?" I said.

So, we both decided to move ahead.

Cautiously and slowly, we started our descent by taking one step at a time. After about ten steps, I suddenly let out an "OMG" scream and fell on my back, sliding uncontrollably down this steep hill, feet first. My vision blurred out, and my heart throbbed like someone was beating a drum in my chest.

I was trying to reach left and right with both hands, looking for something to grab on and seeing if Bill was sliding down too. Then I heard his voice: "There is a small tree in front of you. Grab on!"

I looked down and saw a tree closing in on me. I felt a sharp pain as I frantically straddled it, knowing it was a "do-or-die" situation now and that if I didn't grab it, I would further roll down and hurt myself badly.

Bill yelled, "Hold on, Giorgo. I am coming down to help you."

My *sakouli* got loose and was rolling down the hill. I stayed there motionless, waiting for Bill to get down to help me get off this tree and hopefully walk down to the bottom together. He kept talking to me as he slowly and carefully stepped down so he wouldn't slide to the bottom before me.

I was very uncomfortable, still holding on to the tree with no way to get out of it without help. Soon, I saw Bill sitting right next to me.

"Don't move," he said. He was checking me out, looking for any visible injuries, and asked me, "How are you feeling?"

I said, "Besides some bodily pain, I feel a little dizzy."

He said, "Thank God for this tree."

I agreed by nodding my head. He helped me stand up and slowly started stepping down in a zig-zag fashion to avoid another slide as we held on to each other and eventually reached the bottom safely. We looked and found my *sakouli* intact. Luckily, it hadn't burst open and spilled our food all over the place. We took a deep breath and thanked God for saving my life.

We dusted ourselves off and continued our trip, and after about half an hour of walking, I suggested, "Hey, Bill, we should find a shady spot and take a badly needed break."

We started looking for such a place, and soon, Bill spotted a sizeable bushy tree a couple of hundred feet down the road in front of us. We headed there.

We drank some still-cold water from our canteen, looked at each other, and again thanked God that I hadn't gotten injured or killed in that freaky accident that could have resulted in what we were worried about when planning the trip.

We finished our snack of two hard-boiled eggs with bread and Greek goat cheese.

After twenty minutes of rest, we were on the road again. We planned to walk for at least two more hours before we stopped for lunch.

We checked the time by looking at the sun's position—the sun was our watch. That's how we were taught to tell the time of day. The sun

168

was directly above our heads, meaning that it was noontime and time to look for a shady spot to have lunch; we were already feeling a bit hungry and tired.

We came to an open area filled with several tall, large boulders rising from the bare ground that looked like soldiers on a battlefield without guns. Bill and I had seen real soldiers on battlefields with machine guns and real people getting killed, but this was not a battlefield. It was an excellent place to pick one boulder tall enough with plenty of shade for both of us. Bill spotted one with lots of shade. We walked over, put our gear down, scanned the area for unsealed dangers, sat down, and started our lunch.

After we drank some water, I looked and found two pieces of chicken my mother had cooked the night before we left, a bit of fresh bread, and fresh goat cheese. It felt like we were in a vacuum chamber wholly isolated from the world we knew, or maybe we were too tired and were hallucinating—just a thought.

Right after we finished eating, followed by figs and walnuts as our dessert, a frightening and deafening rifle shot suddenly rang out that sounded like a bomb went off. The bullet stroked the side of the boulder close to Bill and recached, grazing my left arm. I felt a sharp pain and immediately placed my right hand where the pain was coming from. "I got shot, Bill!" He looked at me and saw I was holding my left arm. He panicked when he saw blood dripping on the ground, saying, "Giorgo, you are bleeding." I asked him to tear off my undershirt and wrap it around my arm tightly.

Now, we were both panicked and lay flat on the ground, not knowing what to do—running was not a good option. Then another shot rang out as loud as the first one. This time, the bullet hit the ground next to me, forcing the land under us to shake and showering us with dust from the bullet's impact on the ground in front of us.

We were scared to death. Slowly and carefully, we started looking to see where these shots were coming from. We both were trembling with fear of getting killed, thinking about what our mothers and friends had told us about all the dangers of taking this trip. It was like witnessing death up close. I envisioned my mother back home, praying for us to have a safe journey and waiting for my return. I was lost in my thoughts, remembering what our mothers were telling us about the dangers of this trip, but this was not the time to think or reflect; it was survival time, as the pain in my arm was getting more intense.

Minutes later, we saw two guys with rifles standing on top of a hill directly across from us, about 1000 yards, with rifles strapped on their backs. We could not tell if they were Andartes or a couple of thieves looking to rob us.

Then we heard a loud shout, "*Ti thelete edo?*" (Why are you here?)

"We are just two kids going to Flona," I replied.

They shouted back, "Raise your hands and keep them up until we get there."

We stood up with our hands in the air, but I couldn't raise my left hand too high, and I don't know about Bill, but I wet my pants, standing there with one hand higher than the other, as they started walking toward us.

We kept watching them walking down the hill, and after a few minutes, we lost them as they were below our line of vision. Bill turned to me and said, "Maybe we should run now because they can't see us."

I told Bill, "We can't get too far before. they will find and kill us." We both went silent because we realized we had no options other than waiting until they arrived.

I was thinking about stories I had heard about Andartes stopping and robbing people of all their belongings, including food and shoes. I told Bill, "We have to think of a way to save our food because I am sure that is the first thing they want from us. The next is our shoes and possibly our clothing."

Bill started complaining, saying, "The pain in my arms is killing me." He was afraid to lower his hands because the Andartes were soon to get up to us. "I wish these guys would hurry up and get here soon," he said.

Minutes later, they came close enough for us to see that they indeed were Andartes; they had long and dirty beards, worn-out caps with the red communist emblem pined on the hats, and dirty military uniforms, probably stolen from dead Greek soldiers. But that was not our concern right now; survival was!

Finally, they were standing in front of us, looking like a couple of bums with rifles. One asked me, "What happened to your hand?"

"You shot me," I said.

"At least I didn't kill you. Are you in pain?"

"Yes, I am," I said.

"Too bad. We don't have any medicine to ease your pain. Let me see."

He removed my undershirt, and for the first time, I saw my wound. He said, "You were lucky. You will live."

He gave me back my undershirt. The bleeding had stopped, and I noticed the wound was not too deep. I put my undershirt in my pocket for now.

He asked, "Show us your ID's."

We quickly handed our ID's over to them as we were required to have ID's during the occupation. They told us their names; one was Kosta, who seemed to be the leader, and the other one, George.

After they checked the ID's and confirmed our faces, one of them took out a small notebook from his front shirt pocket and wrote down our names and village name, then gave them back to us and told us, "We know Vresthena. We will come to visit both of you as soon as you get back home." That was not good news for us, but we dismissed the thought for now.

They proceeded to frisk us. In the meantime, I almost fainted with the awful stink from their dirty bodies. I wanted to grab my nose, but then I thought it wouldn't be a good idea. And just then, another thought came to my mind: soap and showers are not high on their list to worry about living up in the mountains.

They found the little money we both had hidden in our back pockets in a small pouch, and after they realized it was a small amount, they put it back in our back pockets with a disingenuous remark, saying, "We could have taken this too, but you can use it to buy some food for your return home."

172

When they finished, we were told to put our hands down; they leaned their rifles against the large boulder and ordered us to empty our *sakoulia*. We wasted no time and laid everything on the ground.

They both kneeled and started separating our food into two portions on the ground. I noticed the more significant portion was the one in front of them and the smaller one in front of us. One of them said, "This is for us," pointing to the large portion, "and that is for you, the small portion." Bill and I made sour faces showing our displeasure and disappointment at what we had just witnessed, but there was very little we could do.

They noticed the anger on our faces for losing most of our food. Kosta remarked, "Hey, kids, we could have taken all your food because a lot of us are starving to death up there," pointing to the mountains, "trying to stay alive and fight to protect you and your families." We knew that was a big lie, but we kept our mouths shut.

I asked him, "How are we going to get to Elona and back home with so little food?"

He snapped back at me with a somewhat threatening tone, saying, "Buy more at the monastery with the money we didn't take from you." He picked up his loot and stood up, still staring at us with angry faces.

After all this back and forth with these two robbers, we thought our ordeal was over when the unthinkable happened. "Take your shoes off; let's exchange them," one of them said with a smirk. They then took off their shoes and handed them to us.

Looking over the pair he gave me, I noticed the sad shape these shoes were in. They were worn-out with holes underneath and sides and missing shoelaces. I said, "How am I going to walk with holes under these shoes? The sharp rocks will cut into my feet."

One guy replied in the same mean tone, "The same way we have been walking and fighting for months now."

He started putting my beautiful boots on his dirty, smelly feet, then looked at me with a big smile and said, "Thank you, kid, these are a bit small for me, but are nice and well-made; where did you get them?"

I was too upset to answer him.

His partner looked at my boots on his friend's feet and said, "Oh, boy, they are great; I wish I had a pair like them."

Then they noticed they forgot to take our blankets and proceeded to remove them from the bottom of our *sakoulia* tied tight so that we wouldn't lose them. We were so angry that we didn't have the will to resist their demands; we just wanted this episode to end.

They told us what they could do to us. "We can take you back with us to our camp, take everything you have, have you put on our uniforms, and train you to become fighters like us. But our commander told us to promise you that we will be visiting your houses in Vresthena soon after you return home. We want to make sure you understand why you should join our great organization—ELAS."

They then geared up to leave. Walked away, they said, "You are free to leave now."

We stood silently for a few minutes. It felt like hours of looking at each other, trying to digest what had just happened to us. Finally, we just realized we had almost lost our lives for sure, lost most of our food and shoes. We also lost at least a couple of hours from the schedule to two desperate and brainwashed looters with rifles.

It is a sorrowful story that happened 72 years back, but it seems like it just happened yesterday, and it will remain in my brain until my brain is no more. As a prelude of going to a holy place to pray, we kept our spirits high and tried to erase what happened, at least for now, but it was not comfortable doing. Nevertheless, we thanked God they didn't do the unthinkable—maybe kidnap us.

After a couple of hours of walking and pondering under a scorching summer sun, we decided to take a break, rest, and maybe take that siesta we were planning before the Andartes ambushed and robbed us. I then realized they also took our blankets. Bill said we both had slept on the ground before and kept looking for a shady spot.

We found a shady tree about 100 ft. on the side of the road and sat on the ground as we had no blankets, scanned the area for any possible dangers, drank some not-so-cold water now, and sat to rest our tired bodies and minds. Then, we lay down on the hard ground for a short nap.

When we woke up, we could hear the *Tsingiria* cicadas (small insects the size of a locust, with large eyes and clear feathers covering their bodies), singing their familiar monotonous screeching sounds. A large owl stood on the branch of a tree to our left, hunting for prey and not paying any attention to a couple tired and scared kids.

I continued to span this strange docile area looking for any dangers. Suddenly, my eyes came upon a rather large gray jackal about 300 meters straight ahead, just outside a thick forest, staring at us. I quietly nudged Bill and said, "Get up. Open your eyes now! But do not scream or move."

When he finally opened his eyes, I whispered to him, "Look straight ahead; a jackal is watching us."

With a fearful whispering voice, he said, "What do we do now?"

Jackals are opportunistic predators, feeding on small to medium-sized animals. Generally, they are not dangerous but are known to attack humans in certain situations. After we stared at each other for about ten minutes, the animal turned around and went back into the forest. We were surprised, of course. Who told it to go back? What made it change its mind? The divine spirit was probably helping us because we were on a sacred mission.

Now, we were both fully awake and checked the sun's position to find out the time. It told us it was midafternoon. We were a bit hungry, but we only had a small amount of food left after the Andartes stole most of it. We had to make sure we had enough to last until we reached Elona.

I looked in my *sakouli* using my right hand as my left was still painful, and I fetched the last hard-boiled egg and some bread. Bill was already munching on something, too, as we were eating and trying to figure out how to make the rest of our trip to the monastery and back home.

Scanning the area while eating, Bill noticed something that looked like a fox running across the open field at the edge of the thick forest. He asked me, "What do you think it is?"

"A fox, indeed," I confirmed. "We should not be concerned because foxes always run away from humans," I said. With that, we got up, ready to get back on the road.

We walked for a while, and soon, the sun began making its exit. Before too long, it got dark. It was a full moon, though, so we didn't have to light up our small kerosene lamp. It was bright as day as we continued walking under the moonlight. It was surreal walking under full moonlight silently through an unknown and rather hostile terrain full of thorny bushes and bare, hard ground to walk on.

Often, the small sharp rocks found their way into our bare feet through the holes in the soles of those Andartes' shoes, piercing the bottom of our feet. We had to sit down to use our first aid kit to clean the blood and place a piece of gauze to stop the bleeding and prevent any possible infection. An infection would be the last thing we needed after all that we had endured so far.

It was a peaceful, silent night, with no wolf and jackal cries, only sounds of crickets and the sounds we made stepping on loose, rolling, small rocks. Other times, there was a whooshing sound made by the tall pine trees as they swung from side to side by the wind or water streaming down from the mountains.

It was about midnight now, and I had no idea how far we were from the monastery. I thought it might be a good time to stop and take a few hours of sleep before we continued.

We finally reached the top of a hill and saw bright lights flickering in the distance, maybe one or two kilometers away. After using our grade school math, we figured out those lights had to be coming from the monastery.

We had to decide whether to continue walking till we got to Elona or find a safe spot to lay down and sleep for a few hours, then get up early, fresh and rested, and get there early in the morning, find a restaurant to have our favorite hot breakfast (3–4 scrambled eggs with feta cheese),

Tiganites Patates, (French fries), all mixed together. After Bill gave my suggestion a thought, he said, "Let's stay and get some sleep as we both are tired."

Since we had no blankets, we used our packed clothes, which we were surprised hadn't also been stolen. We lay them on flat ground with our *sakoulia* for pillows and fell asleep.

We were woken up by the cries of jackals at dawn; this time, we thanked them for waking us up. It was a glorious morning in the forest far away from home, and you could smell and hear the tall pines whooshing by the light wind that added to our excitement of finally getting to where we planned to be in Elona.

Elona Monastery

We got up, picked up all the gear (not much now after the looting), and back on the road we went. After a couple of hours of uneventful walking that brought us close to the monastery, we got our first look at this beautiful structure built on the side of a mountain. We soon entered the monastery, a rather large complex structure, bigger than we expected. There were many buildings and several chapels spread around.

We entered the first chapel and came across the chapel's priest, Fr. George, who welcomed us. After telling him our ordeal of getting there, we asked him, "Where can we wash up? And where is the nearest restaurant for breakfast? We are dirty and starving."

After his warm welcome, he checked out our dirty, dusty clothes and poorly worn-out shoes with a curious look. He asked us, "Where have you come from?"

Both Bill and I said in unison, "From Vresthena."

With a smile, he said, "I met many people from Vresthena that made this trip. Most of them were adults riding mules or donkeys, but you are just kids and walked here! God Bless you both."

We did not comment on his apparent surprise at our decision to undertake such a dangerous trip. We knew he was right and had learned how dangerous it was. He told us, "I am a bit surprised about you kids, at such young ages, taking this long and dangerous trip." Later, he also told us, "Hundreds or maybe thousands make these long and longer trips to come and pray in front of Panagia."

Suddenly, Fr. George noticed the red wound on my left arm. "What happened to your arm he asked?"

"Oh, I got shot by the Andartes," I replied.

With a concerned manner, he asked me to follow him. He opened a rear door and walked into the nurse's room, where an elderly nurse

179

greeted us. Father George asked the nurse to check out my bullet wound and then send me back to the chapel.

The nurse looked at my wound and asked me, "How did you get it?" She cleaned my wound and proceeded to give me a shot.

"Ouch! it hurt!" I said.

"Sorry," she replied, "but we must do this to prevent any infections." She then applied some cream, bandaged my arm, and told me not to remove it until I saw my doctor when I return to my village.

I thanked her for her excellent care and concern, and she showed me the way back to the chapel. Fr. George was happy to see that I was taken care of by the chapel's nurse.

He then told us, "Follow me, and I will show you where you can wash and freshen up and change your clothes." We only had a pair of pants and a long-sleeve shirt each that the looters (*Andartes*) hadn't stolen from us.

Elona Chapels

About a hundred feet up a hill, we came to a large reception room with chairs and comfortable sofas and a large men's room with a shower inside. We both thought we had just arrived in heaven and had never been to such a wonderful place before. Then he pointed to where the restaurant was—about a block away. He said, "Let me know if you need more assistance." He then began walking back to his chapel.

As an expected gesture by all Greek Orthodox Christians, we kissed his hand. It was customary when greeting a priest. Before he parted, I asked him, "Please, tell us how to find the chapel where the Panagia icon was so we can pray, for it is the only reason we have walked this far."

He replied with the same smile, "Yes, it is the same reason that everyone comes to Elona. After your breakfast, come to see me, and I will take you there."

Fr. George's welcome was more than we expected to receive visiting Elona. After we washed up, took a shower, and changed into our only clean pair of pants and shirts, we headed directly to this lovely restaurant where we could smell the Greeks cooking before we even walked inside.

Bill asked the waitress in the restaurant, "Are there any stores around to buy shoes to get rid of the worn shoes with now larger holes under the soles?" She pointed toward a shoe store not far from the restaurant, and we both jumped with joy. We each bought one pair of shoes in our size with money in our pockets, and we still had enough left to buy food for our return home.

Now we had some time to walk around and visit a few other chapels before heading back home; we hoped we wouldn't lose our new shoes on the trip back home.

We enjoyed our favorite hot breakfast with plenty of fresh bread and feta Greek cheese. We then headed to Fr. George's chapel, where he took us to the chapel where the *Panagia* icon was displayed.

He was happy to see us again. "Follow me," he said. He walked with us to *Panagia's* chapel, but before returning to his chapel, he told us, "Come to see me once you are done praying."

The *Panagia* Icon

Me standing next to Icon of Panagia

I found this picture in an old album named *OLDIES* that Bill had taken of me but I couldn't find one of him.

It was midday, and we had to get ready for our return home; we remembered to buy enough food and water and some of our favorite snacks—*stragalia* (toasted chickpeas) and sweet raisins. I remember my grandmother Vasilo used to fill my pockets with my favorite toasted deliciously crunchy, salty *stragalia* and savory sweet golden raisins when I visited her.

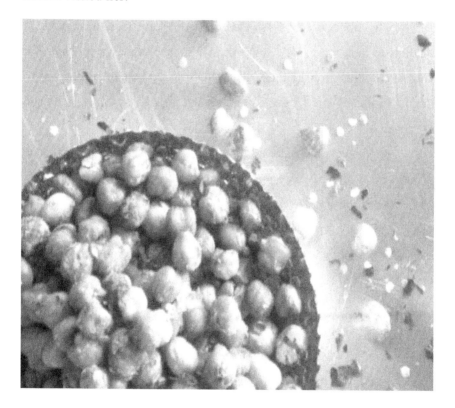

Stragalia **(Toasted Chickpeas)**

Getting Ready to Return Home

When we got everything we needed with the little money we had left, we were ready to get back on the road, once again walking under a scorching hot sun. We thought of waiting till the next early morning, but it was not an option as we had no money left. We started walking on the same road we had come to Elona. While walking Bill commented, "I hope we don't repeat the terrible events we experienced on our way to Elona."

I replied, "I hope not."

After about two hours of the uneventful walk under the hot sun, it was time to look for a shady spot to rest and have some water. Then Bill pointed and said, "Look, Giorgo, that's the spot we stopped on our way to Elona." I looked where he was pointing and agreed it was that spot and proceeded to walk there.

We drank some water, took out our favorite snack—*stragalia* and raisins—enjoyed our twenty-minute break, and then returned to the road.

About an hour later, we came to the intersection of an unpaved road that looked like a motor road, but we didn't remember crossing it on our way to Elona. Maybe we traveled during the night, that's why. Anyhow, just before we started to cross it, we noticed a small truck coming from our left. We stopped to see who the driver was, thinking maybe it was someone we knew.

The driver slowed down, approaching us, then came to a halt in front of us. He was looking at us like he knew us; finally, he said, "I know both of you; what are you doing here?"

To our big surprise, we recognized him too and even remembered his name—Niko.

I said, "We visited Elona. Now, we are returning home."

He asked, "Did you guys walk to Elona? And now you're walking back home?" He had a curious look on his face.

I said, "Yes, Niko."

He said, "I am going home too-- jump in; I will drive you there."

Bill and I looked at each other with big, happy smiles and sat next to him in the front of the cab a bit tight and pulled the door shut. No complaints, you know.

His truck started winding as he was changing shifts on our way home. Riding in a truck instead of walking this time was a lucky break for us. Maybe our prayers had begun working.

We told Niko all about our trip adventures on our way to Elona.

Having listened to us, he expressed his concerns, saying, "You were lucky you came through unharmed. You must not try to do it again, especially these days when there is a war going on," he warned us.

We both agreed we were lucky; it was really a risky trip for a couple of kids, but I felt only kids could do stupid things like that.

Niko dropped us off at the platia. He would have gladly driven us to our homes, but there was no road for cars those days.

We thanked Niko for the much-needed ride and walked home as our mothers were worried about us.

Chapter 14:
The Defeat of the Communist
Guerillas

The Greek Civil War began soon after the Nazi withdrawal from Greece. For the KKE, the Greek communist party, this was a long-awaited opportunity – first, to be the Greek resistance to the occupation, and then to take control of the country after the war was over and deliver it to their bosses, the Russians.

The German evacuation left ELAS, the country's largest communist organization, in charge. Having wiped out the remnants of the security battalions that had been appointed by the Nazi collaborationist administration, they proceeded to terrorize the Peloponnesus with a series of atrocities, leading the inhabitants of the islands to a complete surrender.

When the British forces arrived, they discovered that ELAS, led by Zervas, had total control of Greece, with the lone exception of Epiros. After the ELAS fighters learned that their leaders had signed an agreement with the exiled ministers of King George II that limited their representation in the new parliament to only four seats, they became enraged. As a result, a bloodbath occurred on December 3, 1944, igniting a civil war unlike any seen in Europe for the next half-century.

At this point, the British and Greek police were battling to keep order in a city that was riddled with pain from the war's devastations. Angry citizens marched into the city's center shortly after daybreak. Protesters, many of them women, rushed into the center square and focused on the apartment of Greek Prime Minister George Papandreou.

A grenade exploded among the crowd of protesters as they stormed the building. Protesters marched up and down the street, waving British and American flags.

Overwhelmed officers began to retreat from the mob until an armed officer emerged from the station and screamed, "Shoot the scum!" and, kneeling, opened fire on the crowd. The other police officers followed suit. The protesters stampeded; 12 civilians were killed, and many more injured. British paratroopers were ordered not to intervene, but they stood uncomfortably nearby as the events unfolded.

Leftist revolutionaries, mainly communists and supporters of the deposed dictatorship of Ioannis Metaxas, were opposing the occupying forces by 1942, as were other conservative and anti-imperialist factions in the country. It was only when more groups joined the National Liberation Front (EAM) that the National Popular Liberation Army (NPLA) was formed (ELAS). Even while they battled the Axis, ELAS eliminated other opposing factions.

The EAM was resisted by the Greek government in exile, as well as the collaborationist government, which established well-equipped security units. In anti-partisan actions, these forces incurred significantly more casualties than the Germans or the Italians.

The National Greek Republican League, or EDES, was an anti-communist resistance group that opposed the monarchist government in exile. Because the EDES battled both the EAM and the occupying forces, the British secretly funded and equipped it.

The savage civil war of 1946-49 in Greece between the KKE and the royalist government, restored by referendum in 1946, concluded in the postwar tensions between the Western and Communist worlds.

The Communist spearhead was the so-called Democratic Army of Greece, organized in the northern mountains by Markos Vafiadis, a former resistance leader, and preyed on the local villages with disastrous results. Thousands of young children were taken and sent to communist countries to be taught as Marxist-Leninists, while men and women were forced to join their fight against the Greek army.

Markos received great support from the communist regimes in Yugoslavia, Albania, and Bulgaria. In contrast, the royalist government received arms, equipment, and massive assistance from the Americans, who believed Stalin backed the KKE. However, the Greek communists themselves complained angrily about Moscow's lack of support.

On August 1, the Government forces overpowered the guerillas in their trenches. They destroyed them in hand-to-hand fighting, and government forces conquered most of the guerilla positions atop the Grammos mountain range within a week.

In the 1948 split between Stalin and Tito, the KKE made a major error by siding with Moscow. As a result, Yugoslavia's help was cut off. Following intense internal squabbles, Markos was expelled as a "defeatist" and replaced by Nikos Zakhariadis, the KKE's veteran Moscow-trained secretary-general.

Tito closed his border to the Democratic Army in July 1949. Within a month, government forces with artillery and air support effectively destroyed the Democratic Army in the Grammos mountains on the Albanian border. The rebels fought valiantly, and several locations were defended to the death. Most of the remaining communists fled to Albania, and on October 16, the KKE proclaimed on its "Free Greek" radio that its forces had temporarily halted operations to prevent the "total devastation" of Greece. Zakhariadis was deposed as Secretary-General in 1956 and spent the rest of his life in exile in Siberia, where he died.

In his book *Eleni*, author Nickolas Gage says, "In the summer of 1948, guerillas and government forces fought to possess the peak Grammos, the guerillas' major stronghold. The government forces fought the guerillas on the slopes of Mount Kleftis and eventually took control of the summit, only to be forced back by a daring guerilla counter-offensive."

Villagers, including women and older boys, battled valiantly, eager to lay down their lives for the ultimate victory of the Greek people's freedom. There was no time to bury the remains that were scattered across the cliffs, and the odor of dead bodies became terrible in the blazing July sun. On the other hand, the Greek leaders were dead set on capturing the peak at all costs.

When his field commanders advised a brief withdrawal, Commander Tsakalotos said, "Do not retreat half a meter. Even if it takes the entire Army Corps, Kleftis will be taken." On July 31, the government forces bombed the summit of Kleftis with 20,000 artillery shells in preparation for a decisive assault.

In the rear, King Paul, and Queen Frederica, as well as the commander of the American mission, James Van Fleet, paid visits to the troops to encourage them to fight and win. Battalion 583 reached the summit of Kleftis around 4:30 a.m.

Between 1946 and 1949, the Greek government's armed forces suffered roughly 48,000 casualties; their armed opponents likely suffered half that many. Thousands of civilians were killed by death squads on both sides, and many more perished because of violence, disease, and malnutrition. The civil war may have claimed the lives of as many as 158,000 Greeks. The economic damage in Greece was similarly devastating, but the Marshall Plan would lay the groundwork for recovery.

Greeks were able to take advantage of a massive American military commitment after 1948, which shifted the balance in their favor. The Greek government was able to push the guerillas one way into Albania with the help of American equipment and training, including surplus Curtiss Helldivers.

With the decisive and massive American commitment to free Greece from communism, the Greek government won the civil war, and Greece once again remained a free democratic country. The Greek people erected a 12-foot golden bronze statue in Athens, Greece, to honor President Truman for his courageous action and insight.

The Truman Doctrine, 1947

President Harry S. Truman developed the Truman Doctrine, which stated that the US would provide political, military, and economic help to any democratic nation threatened by external or internal authoritarian forces. The Truman Doctrine effectively shifted US foreign policy from one of withdrawal from regional wars that did not directly involve the US to one of prospective intervention in far-flung conflicts.

The Truman Doctrine was born out of President Harry S. Truman's speech to a joint session of Congress on March 12, 1947. The speech was prompted by the British government's recent statement that, as of March 31, "it would cease to provide military and economic support to the Greek government in its civil war against the Greek Communist Party." Truman requested that Congress back the Greek government in its fight against the communists. He also requested assistance from Congress in the case of Turkey, which had hitherto relied on British aid.

The US government felt that the Soviet Union supported the Greek Communist war effort at the time and was concerned that if the communists won the civil war in Greece, the Soviets would eventually influence Greek policy. In truth, Soviet leader Joseph Stalin had deliberately withheld support from the Greek Communists, forcing Yugoslav Prime Minister Josip Tito to do the same, to the damage of Soviet-Yugoslav ties. However, President Truman's choice to actively assist Greece and Turkey was impacted by a variety of other foreign policy issues.

The withdrawal of British help to Greece provided the essential spark for the Truman administration to realign American foreign policy, given the deteriorating relationship with the Soviet Union and the appearance of Soviet intervention in Greek and Turkish affairs. As a result, President Truman proposed in his speech that Congress send $400 million in aid to the Greek and Turkish governments and support the transfer of American civilian and military people and equipment to the region.

Truman had two justifications for his request. He warned that a Communist triumph in the Greek Civil War would jeopardize Turkey's political stability, putting the Middle East's political stability in jeopardy. This could not be tolerated, given the region's enormous strategic importance to US national security. Truman also stated that the US was obligated to support "free people" in their fight against "totalitarian governments" because the growth of authoritarianism would "undermine the basis of world peace and thereby the US' security." It became "the policy of the United States to help free peoples who were opposing attempted enslavement by armed minorities or by foreign influences," as the Truman Doctrine put it.

True to his words, Truman contended that the United States could no longer stand by and let the coercive extension of Soviet tyranny into free, independent nations because American national security now rested on more than the physical protection of American land. The Truman Doctrine, on the other hand, pledged the United States to actively support democratic countries in the preservation of their political integrity, where such an offer was regarded to be in the best interest of the United States.

American approval and delivery of cash, combat weapons and training to Greek forces ended in August 1949 at the ridge of Mount Grammos near the Albanian border, the final major communist stronghold. After days of ferocious fighting, the rebels finally surrendered, escaping across the Albanian border. The last of the rebel forces were wiped off during the final assault on Mount Grammos, aided by Helldivers dropping napalm. After Stalin ordered the Greek communists to proclaim a truce, the fighting swiftly subsided.

Chapter 15:
The Wourna (Reservoir) Story

This is another story which nearly brought us close to a tragic death as we pursued the freedom to play like kids as we used to before the Nazi invasion and occupation.

In addition to my two childhood best friends, Taki, and Themis, I also became close friends with my second cousin, the same Bill Blathras who walked with me to the monastery Elona.

We used to collect and play marbles on the dirt ground. Each of us had a stash of colorful marbles of various bright colors, and we bragged about the quantity and color variations each one of us owned because they were the only toys our parents could afford to buy for us at that time. Things like toy cars or bikes and other expensive toys like some kids were fortunate to have our parents could not afford to buy for us.

There was no swimming or fishing in the area around our village; we were more than 50 miles from the nearest beach, so playing or merely walking on the beach was only a dream for us. Instead, during the hot summer months, we had to look for a puddle or basin of water deep enough to jump in and cool off, which also gave us a reason to get out of our homes.

There were many *wournes* (reservoirs) in and near the village, some of them quite small, but many over five feet deep when full of water. People would build a *wourna* near a garden or a farm to collect water captured from mountains, streams, or in some cases, rivers, so the gardeners could water their tomato and vegetable plants and farmers water their crops. Most of these *wournes* were too deep for most of us who didn't know how to swim.

One bright, hot summer morning, we came to our parents with a simple request.

"Can we go swimming in a *wourna* not too far away?"

The adults were dubious about such an expedition, and rightly said so.

"Where is this *wourna*?" one of the parents asked.

"Not too far. Bill knows where it is."

All eyes turned to Bill.

"It's not far," Bill confirmed. "Just a half-hour walk down the hill."

"A half-hour? You're sure?"

"No more than that. I know how to get there. There's a path."

Reluctantly, the parents agreed.

"Stick together," they admonished us. "Go straight there, don't wander off the path, and watch out for Germans, *andartes*, and wild animals. Be careful, and don't do anything stupid."

It was great luck. Bill had managed to persuade the grown-ups that it was okay for us to go.

What he had forgotten to mention was how steep this small hill was, how full of thorny bushes the winding paths were, how many sharp rocks we had to avoid stepping on, the number of venomous snakes lying concealed along the way, or that we might run into a German or *andartes* checkpoint and get shot. No, none of us was about to worry about these dangers; the only thing in our young minds was how fast we could get to the *wourna*.

We each put a few of our usual snacks in our pockets – walnuts, chestnuts, and figs – and headed barefoot down the steep hill toward the *wourna*, hoping it was full of water and unguarded against crazy kids like us, who might accidentally open the water trapdoor and waste the incredibly needed water collected in this *wourna* for the sole purpose of watering some farmer's plants.

We were running down the winding path like goats being pursued by wolves when, suddenly, a large rabbit sprang from the bushes like a small deer, scared by our loud voices and the sound of rocks rolling from under our feet, and ran across our narrow path and into the woods.

Bill cried out, "Oh, my God! This rabbit almost ran into me!"

Taki and I turned to see what had happened, but the rabbit had disappeared into the woods.

We kept walking down the hill until Taki spotted a long black snake wiggling across our path. It did not seem threatening, but we all stopped and watched it go into the thick brown bushes. Then we continued walking and, sometimes, sliding down the hill.

After twenty minutes of running and sliding, we arrived at the bottom of the hill into a ravine where we could hear and see the crystal-clear water streaming toward the main river. The birds, along with the summer *Tsingiria*, cicadas were singing as though to welcome us to their sanctuary.

It was a beautiful moment even for teenagers like us, in a hurry to get to the (hopefully full) *wourna* and cool off a bit by jumping into it.

As we were walking on a path through a thick line of low-level trees, we saw two men walking toward us with their rifles poking up behind their heads wearing round black hats. We all stopped, trying to see if they were Germans or *andartes*; then Taki said, "They are *andartes*. I recognize their caps." By this point, they were in full view and looking all around; perhaps they wanted to make sure we were alone. Then we spotted two more behind them; one was carrying a Thompson machine gun as we all knew what a Thomson machine gun looked like. They kept walking cautiously toward us, with one hand behind their backs, keeping a wary grip on their rifles, ready to turn them on us if they felt threatened in any way.

I was first in line, so I was the first one they spoke to.

"What's your name?" the man asked. "And what are you doing down here alone?"

"I'm George."

"George what?"

"Kakridas."

"Kakridas. From Vresthena?"

"Yes, sir." We know your father.

"Well, what are you doing here?"

"We are planning to go swimming in the *wourna* you just walked by," I stammered. "Honest."

Both soldiers shook their heads.

"Your parents let you kids come this far, knowing the area is crawling with Germans?"

There wasn't much we could say to that, so we didn't say anything.

"Well, have you seen any Germans around?"

"No, no, no," we all said together. "You are the first people we've seen."

They seemed to be in a hurry, and all four continued walking past us, and then one turned around and said, "Go back home now. The German patrols come through here at about this time."

Then they disappeared up the ravine.

We looked at each other like a bunch of scared rabbits with fear on our faces.

"Maybe we should go home," I said.

"Yes, let's," Bill said.

"But we're almost there now," Taki said.

"How far is it now, Bill?" Themis asked.

"A couple of hundred yards."

"That's it?" Taki said. "Come on. We've come this far. Let's just go swimming for a little while; then we can go home."

Now we could see the *wourna* – it was full to the top with muddy water. We all ran and stood at the edge for a few seconds, then we removed our clothes and threw them all over the place as though we would never need them again.

Taki dove in first to test the water; he stuck his head up above the surface and said, "It's cool! Come on – jump in!"

We were careful not to take deep dives because there was zero visibility, and we didn't know what sharp objects—like broken trees or rocks—rolled down from the hill above and might be lying on the muddy bottom.

The muddy water was about six feet deep, and none of us knew how to swim well; in fact, we could float only when our heads were underwater, and though we tried hard not to swallow any water, Bill did, and started coughing hard. He had to get out and sit on the edge of the *wourna* for several minutes before jumping in again.

After enjoying the water for some time, I stuck my head up above the surface and said, "Guys, shouldn't we be getting back home as the *andartes* told us to?"

Everyone agreed, and we got out of the *wourna* and started looking around for our clothes, which we had so hastily discarded on the edge of the *wourna*. But they weren't there!

In a rising panic, we searched the ground all around us, covering the same area repeatedly, growing ever more alarmed at the thought that someone had stolen our clothes. Was someone playing a joke on us? Was one of us playing a joke on the others? If so, it wasn't funny. There was nothing funny about being found by the Germans like this, naked at the bottom of a ravine.

Suddenly, we heard a loud, angry voice coming from the south side of the *wourna*. We turned around, facing an old man walking toward us, holding our clothes with one hand and a heavy stick with the other. He shouted, "You little bastards! What are you doing in my *wourna*? Get the hell out and go home now! If I ever catch you in my *wourna* again, not only will I not give your clothes back, but I will make sure you all go to jail!"

We all stood there with our mouths opened and our hearts pounding as we watched the old man throw our clothes on the muddy ground and yelled, "Go home!" We all looked at each other with regret and a bit of shame for not following the rules and respecting other people's property, but we had learned our lesson. Thus ended our *wourna* dream of fun – with a mixture of excitement and disappointment.

The only good thing about the day's adventure was the feeling of bravery in having dealt with many natural and manmade dangers. We felt a little more equipped to survive in a world full of daily dangers under the occupation of a brutal enemy, the Nazis, than we had that morning. Still, we began our walk back home with our heads down.

This was a badly needed diversion from our very difficult daily life under the occupation and the *andartes* controlling every moment of our lives, but we did not know the many dangers we would face on the way home.

Rather than running down the steep hill as we had done on our way to the *wourna*, we were now slowly walking up the same steep hill.

"Ouch!" Taki shouted as he sat down, holding his left foot.

"What happened?" we all said.

"I sliced the bottom of my foot," Taki replied. "And it is bleeding."

He ripped a piece off his undershirt and wrapped it around his foot, and we continued walking, but now he was limping and couldn't run even if he had to.

We were about a third of the way home when a loud rifle shot suddenly rang out from down below in the ravine; it was followed by a second that reverberated through the mountains and sounded like many shots. That frightened us, and we had to drop to the hard ground. We had no idea where the shots had come from, but I remembered the four *andartes* we had met on our way to the *wourna*; they might have run into a German patrol. As they had told us, this area was crawling with Germans.

More machine guns and rifle fire rang out; suddenly, it sounded like we were in a war zone. A loud thump made me jump; a stray bullet had slammed into the ground next to my right shoulder. That made me think we had to move further up the hill because we could easily be killed lying so close to a raging battle.

Another barrage of machine gun fire frightened us still more, and we all looked around to find a large rock to hide behind and avoid being hit. There was another burst of machine gun fire, followed by a large explosion like a grenade or a mortar shell.

"We've got to move," I whispered to the others. "But we can't stand up and run because they might take us for the enemy on the run and start shooting."

I could read in their faces what remained unsaid: if that happened, they would probably kill one and maybe all of us.

"So, we must move on our bellies," I went on, "like soldiers do when they're under attack."

They all agreed and began wiggling like that snake we saw on the way down; when we thought we had moved far enough, we could stand up and run fast like rabbits, but with our heads down.

Another stray bullet slammed next to Taki, missing his head by inches; he was lagging behind us because of his injured foot. We urged him to try to move faster.

"Let's stand up and run," Bill said. "We are probably far enough now."

Like we knew how far we were from the battlefield and how far we had to be safe from bullets! But I remembered from coming down that there was a ridge which we could go over, in which case we would be safe at least from direct fire from down below.

"Let's keep crawling until we get over that ridge," I said. "Then they won't be able to shoot up at us, at least."

We kept wiggling like snakes, and we were just about to go over the ridge when Themis let out a scream. We turned around to see what had happened: he was holding the index finger of his right hand.

"I was stung by a scorpion!" he screamed, then kept on screaming very loudly as he was pounding on the scorpion with a stone...

There was nothing we could do to help with the pain, but I had been stung by a scorpion once myself, and I knew it was very painful, but it wasn't fatal.

"You are not going to die from a scorpion sting," I said. "It just hurts a lot. There's nothing we can do about it now, but it'll just go away on its own. You're not in real danger of dying from the sting; it's the bullets you must worry about. So, you had better start crawling again; the pain will fade soon. However, I did not tell him that it would take at least 24 hours for the pain to stop, as I knew all too well from when I'd been stung. But now was not the time to give Themis the bad news.

Somehow, we reached the ridge without further incident and stopped to rest for a few minutes; when we resumed, we would probably be running upright, so we needed a bit of refreshment. We shared a few leftover snacks that had survived our *wourna* encounter; all the while, we could hear bullets whizzing over our heads. But they were flying high up from us; their trajectory meant that we were safe unless a bullet hit a rock and ricocheted toward us, which would be such bad luck as even we had not seen that day.

By the time we got moving again, the battle rage seemed to have slowed down, but single rifle shots still whistled through the tree leaves above us from time to time. We had to keep moving as fast as we could, and maybe faster than we thought, so we could get away from this dangerous situation. When we were about ten minutes from my house, we decided to make a run up the hill.

"Let's keep our heads down and run," I said.

We agreed, but were concerned about Taki – with his foot injury, he might not be able to keep up with us.

"How do you feel about running?" I asked him.

"It hurts a lot when I step on it," he replied, "but I will try my best."

"Okay. Let's go! And keep your heads down!"

I jumped on my feet with my head down and started running up the hill on the same winding and full-of-rocks path.

Suddenly, we heard screams.

"Help! Help, I'm hit!"

It sounded like Taki's voice. We looked back, but we couldn't see him, and the screams grew louder. Themis was closest to him and ran back to look for Taki, only to find him screaming in agony. Taki's kneecap had been shot, and he was trying to stop the blood, which was gushing like a water fountain.

"He's been shot! Come fast!" Themis yelled in shock as he was still crying from the scorpion sting.

I ran toward them and wrapped my undershirt around Taki's knee to momentarily stop the bleeding.

"We need to take him to a doctor in the village and then to a hospital in Sparta," I said. "He needs to be warm, and we have to make sure he doesn't move."

I ran up the hill like a rabbit – maybe faster – to get my parents. My mother was washing clothes but immediately looked up when she saw me panting and out of breath.

"What happened?" Her voice was laced with worry.

"Taki's been shot. They blew his kneecap off. We need to get him to the village doctor."

She dropped the soap and the *copano* (clothes beating stick) and yelled for my father, who was working among the grapevines. He came running.

"What is it? What happened?" he said.

"We have to go and get Taki," I said, panting. "His kneecap's been blown away by a bullet from the battle down in the ravine."

Immediately, my father fetched our mule, Truman, and told me to get on. We rode down the hill to where Taki was lying on the ground, hoping he had recovered from the shock. When we got there, Taki was awake but in immense pain. I jumped off Truman, and we were trying to figure out how to get him on the mule without causing more injuries to his knee, but we had few options, and the only viable one was for my father to get on Truman while we handed Taki to him so he could hold his foot straight.

All three of us picked him up, and he started screaming loudly again, but we managed to lift him up to my father's arms. He couldn't keep his knee straight, but there was nothing we could do about that; Truman was not an ambulance.

It took us 15 minutes or so to get to the doctor's office with Truman trotting all the way, although my father knew how to make him trot faster. Taki was unresponsive; he jounced and jolted with the mule's gait, but it looked like he'd passed out.

"He's alive," my father said, seeing my stricken face. "He's just gone into shock. He'll be okay. We must get him to the doctor; the doctor will revive him, then transfer him to a hospital in Sparta by car."

Themis couldn't stand the scorpion sting pain and went home. We finally reached the doctor's office; Bill and I stayed there with my father, waiting to hear from the doctor. We were relieved when he reappeared; he looked like he had good news, or at least like he didn't have the worst news.

"I was able to stop the bleeding," he announced, "and gave him medication to stop the pain. A car is going to come and take him to a hospital in Sparta as soon as possible; the boy needs surgery."

"Can we see him?" I asked.

"Yes. In fact, you can go into my office and talk to him if you'd like. Just don't tire him out too much."

"You'll be okay when you get to the hospital, Taki," I told him. "We'll be waiting for you to come home."

Taki managed to crack a smile at that, and when the car came to take him away, he waved goodbye to us. In the meantime, the church bells started ringing the alarm; it meant the Germans were coming.

"Let's hurry home," my father said, "before the Nazis arrive."

But of course, he could not stay in the village. He needed to go back to the caves.

Chapter 16:
The Aftermath of the Civil War

At the end of the civil war, the streets and fields were littered with unexploded ammunition left behind from the battles between the Greek Army and the *andartes*. Unfortunately, that became a large problem in our village, especially for the children. Several young kids from our school were killed when they found unexploded munitions on the ground and thought they were toys to play with or tried to pull them out of the ground, only for them to explode in their hands. I knew two such kids quite well. In fact, the same thing almost happened to me and my longtime friends: Taki, Themis, and Bill.

It was a beautiful sunny day and my name day, *Agiou Gergiou*, or St. George's Day, when all Georges celebrate their name day and invite all who can do so to come to our house for a glass of retsina wine, *mezedes*, (appetizers), *Glyka-- Kourambiedes* or *diples* dipped in honey.

Agios Georgios, the church, was only a ten-minute walk down the narrow, dusty road. Sometimes, we could hear the liturgy hymns from our house. Today, my mother told my sister and me to get ready for church.

"Giorgo, put on your new pants and shoes that Uncle Gus sent you," she said, referring to the gifts I'd received from my uncle in America. "And make sure you wash your face and brush your teeth."

My sister was always slow in getting ready, and we had to wait for her. Half an hour later she was finally ready, and we started walking down the cement stairs and down the dusty road, which was full of small stones, being extra careful not to fall and dirty our clean new clothes. Minutes later, we arrived at the church and were surprised to see a line of people waiting to enter the church. We, too, stood in line.

"Happy name day, Giorgo!"

I turned around to see who had wished me happy name day; I saw Taki with his mother. He was waving and smiling. I waved back as we entered the church, and afterward, we all lit a candle and did our cross; we could not walk too far as the small church was full of standing parishioners, as there were no seats to sit. I saw Taki and Themis standing with their parents, and we winked and smiled at each other; then Bill entered and stood next to Taki and Themis. We had planned to play soccer in the afternoon before my name-day reception in the evening.

When the liturgy was over, everyone shook my hand and wished me happy name day, and I reminded them all that we were celebrating, and everyone was invited to stop by and enjoy *Glyka* (sweets) that my mother had made. Then we all walked back home.

There, we enjoyed a special dinner my mother had cooked for my name day—baked (in our brick oven) chicken with potatoes. I could smell the aroma even as we were climbing the stairs.

After my special dinner and a lot of wishes and kisses for my name day, I told my family I was meeting Taki, Themis, and Bill.

"We're going to play soccer on top of the hill," I said, referring to the hill over our house. "I'll make sure to be back in time for my name day celebration."

"Be careful," my mother said, as always. "Don't hurt yourself."

We did get injured sometimes playing soccer, but I wasn't thinking of that as I headed out through the *apothiki* (storage room) and back door. I was full of good feelings on account of it being my name day and meeting my friends to play soccer.

Taki and Themis were both waiting for me at the top of the hill; Bill came and apologized for being a bit late, and Taki, although he could not run yet because of his knee injury, had even brought his real ball. I noticed that the ball needed some air pumped into it, but we did not have a pump; even so, the game was on. Taki could not run but he and Themis alternated as goal keepers, and the game began. Themis was the goalkeeper this time and kicked the ball to us. Bill stopped the ball and passed it to me; I dribbled on the hard ground—there was no grass on this sun-drenched hill we called *Alataria*—and I was sure of a goal. With a hard right kick, the ball passed Themis' right hand and rolled down the hill behind him.

Themis ran after the ball, but before he was about to stop it with his right foot, he tripped and fell hard on the hard ground, face down, and started screaming. He was clutching his right leg and seemed to be in pain. I ran to see what had happened to him; we could hear him crying and saying something but couldn't understand what he was saying.

Taki said, "I think he said he broke his leg."

When I reached him, I asked him to lie on his back, took my shirt off, folded it up, and placed it under his head.

"Try not to move your leg," I said. "And stop crying."

Neither one of us knew what to do other than make him comfortable until we could get help.

Taki and I stayed with him for a while until he seemed to calm down and stopped crying. Then we both helped him off his feet, but he couldn't step on his right foot; it was hurting.

"Fetch the ball, Bill," I said, "and help me carry him back."

We started walking back with Themis leaning on both of us with his right foot off the ground. Then, suddenly, Themis yelled out, "Look! That's what tripped me!"

He pointed to a gray metal object sticking out of the ground. We took another step, so we could see what it was. Themis stooped down to get a closer look; I kept supporting Themis, helping him stay off his bad foot.

After looking at the mysterious object for a few seconds, Themis said, "I think it looks like the picture our teacher showed us in the school of a live mortar shell."

It was sunken into the ground at an angle with only the fins exposed; it was those fins that had tripped Themis.

"Don't touch it," I said. "Remember what the teacher told us about what happens when we handle live ammunition."

Nevertheless, I was fascinated, and upon taking a closer look, I could confirm Taki's observation that it did indeed look like an unexploded mortar shell. We were about to keep walking back when, suddenly, a man's voice came from behind us, and we turned to see an old man with his donkey loaded with cut wood for his cooking stove. "*Ti kanete eki Pedia?*" the old man asked. "What are you kids doing there?"

He and his donkey drew closer to see what we were looking at; then, when he was close enough to see, he shouted, "All of you, run as fast as you can and hide behind that rock!" He pointed to a tall rock next to the maple tree. "And stay there until I tell you to move. I must remove it from the ground safely."

We obeyed instantly, following his instructions to the letter, except for the part about running – we couldn't run because we had to carry Themis on our shoulders, but we were quick enough. The urgency in his voice had suddenly brought home to us the gravity of our situation.

"Mister!" we called from behind the cover of the rock. "What's your name?"

"Gianni!" came the faint reply.

We huddled down behind the rock, horrified at the thought of what could have happened when Themis tripped over the live shell and still more horrified at what might yet happen to this old man, Gianni, if he tried to remove it.

We took turns peeking from behind the rock to check on Gianni. He was on the ground, using an axe he had pulled off the donkey; he was carefully digging around the shell, picking away at the dirt and rock in which it was buried. Several horrifying minutes went by until we peeked again and saw that he had cleared about a meter around the shell, and he was standing and wiping the sweat off his face; we were sure it wasn't from the scorching heat of the sun. It was the possibility that this could be the last day of his life.

A few horrified minutes later, we peeked again, and Gianni was holding with both hands a long and heavy live shell.

"You can go home now," he shouted at us, "and I will take this to the police station. And remember when you find anything metal that looks like a shell or hand grenade, you should never touch or try to remove it from the ground; just go and tell the police about it."

Later, we found out that Gianni was in the Greek Army, and he was trained to handle unexploded ammunition.

Before we ran back home, we stood there looking at each other for a while, motionless, with no words coming out of our mouths. Our silence spoke of how close we had come to joining the list of so many other kids who had met their deaths by playing with deadly toys the war had left behind.

Themis was still in pain, so we decided to take him to his house and have his parents take him to the doctor and check his foot. His parents panicked when they saw us helping him to walk; they wanted to know what had happened. I told them. His mother screamed and crossed herself, thanking God for saving her boy. His father immediately helped him onto his truck and sped toward the doctor in the square. We asked his mother to let us know what the doctor said and reminded her to come to my name day party.

"And be sure to bring Themis if he's okay," I added.

Bill and Taki walked home, and I walked home alone, sad that my friend was injured and might not be able to come to celebrate my name day, but extremely happy that none of us were killed by the live shell.

This is another story on my "never-forget" list. God must have been watching over us and whispering in our ears: "Hey, dumb kids, I don't need you up here yet; do not touch that shell and go home while you are still alive and tell your mothers what happened so they can warn other mothers about how to save their children and what to do when they find live ammunition."

I was elated when I saw all my friends come to my name-day party with their parents. The doctor had told Themis that he, fortunately, did not have any broken bones, just an ankle sprain; he was on crutches now but in good spirits.

I could not miss my best friend's name day," Themis whispered in my ear. "Nor your mother's *Glyka*."

However, children continued to find and play with live ammunition on and off the streets, and several died before the villagers pressured the school principal to run classes aggressively and to educate the children on how to avoid such dangerous situations. The mayor urged all the villagers to participate in this effort, join in the search for explosives, and notify the police to safely remove them.

Unfortunately, we never learned and continued to play with handmade guns and live ammunition found on the streets and fields. We used to throw live rifle shells in the fire and stand behind small bushes and hear the explosions and the bullets whizzing by our heads, but fortunately, they didn't find any one of our heads. We made wooden handguns and played soldiers battling the *andartes*; guns were the only toys for us to play with.

One time, I took my father's revolver and a dozen shells to the farm in Vambakies and practiced trying to hit our favorite olive tree. After several shots, I managed to put a bullet in the old tree trunk about three meters from the ground, but the bullet did not exit the thick trunk, and I

213

forgot to cover the entry hole with mud, so it was still visible. My father might see it and start asking questions like, "Who shot our favorite olive tree?" I would be in serious trouble.

A few days later, my father did notice the hole in the tree, and after he walked around and saw there was no exit hole, he knew it was a pistol, not a rifle bullet, and I detected he was shaking his head, which made me a bit nervous. I heard him muttering, "Who in the hell was shooting at our olive tree with a pistol?"

"Probably the *chites* did," I offered, though he hadn't asked me. "I heard they went through this area a few days ago. Who else would do such a thing – shooting at our olive tree?"

He looked at me and shook his head again.

"Go finish your planting."

Somehow, I got the feeling he didn't believe me. When he discovered the missing shells, he probably suspected that it was me, but he never mentioned it to me again.

Taki and I were not through with our gun adventures yet, and we were often to be found playing with pretend handmade wooden guns. One day, we came up with the idea of going on a shooting spree; he could steal shells from his uncle, and I would bring my father's shotgun. We planned to do it as soon as he was able to get the shells when his uncle wasn't around. A couple of days later, he came over to my house with a bag full of shotgun shells. While my mother was busy weaving on her *Argalio*, I took the shotgun, and we both walked up to the top of the hill we called Alataria. That was the same hill we almost died on when Taki tripped on a live shell. I was holding my father's 12-gauge double-barrel shotgun, and Taki was carrying two bags—one full of cans and bottles for targets and the other full of shotgun shells. We felt like we were going into battle, like real soldiers—the same hill where we were almost killed by tripping over a live mortar shell; we were now doing target practice with live shotgun shells.

In the middle of this hill stood an old maple tree. I had been told that this tree must be over two hundred years old and had survived bad weather and many wars, from the Ottomans to the Nazis and now the Greek Civil War, and it was still standing, watching a couple of kids do target practice with a shotgun using live shells. If it could talk, the old tree would tell us to go home to our mothers and stop playing with guns. But trees can't talk, so we were getting ready to play.

At the foot of this old tree was a large rock where we placed our targets: a bottle or a can on the same spot the Greek soldiers used to take cover from machine gun fire from the *andartes* on another hill about a kilometer away, as the civil war was raging on. But today, this huge rock was used for our target practice.

Taki placed the first target, an empty orange juice can, on the rock and moved a few feet away but not too far because he wanted to hear the pellets whizz by his face before hitting the target. Not too smart, but what do you expect from kids that lived where bullets were always whizzing by and who were somehow still alive?

I took my position about 35 feet away, aimed, and pulled the trigger; the can disappeared. Taki went after the broken can; he examined the damage trying to count the number of holes in the almost demolished can. I decided to move back another ten feet, and Taki placed another can on the rock and moved away again. I aimed and fired; the target remained intact, but it looked like Swiss cheese.

Now it was Taki's turn. He took the same spot; I placed a bottle on the rock and moved behind Taki as I was not interested in hearing the pellets whizzing by me. Taki aimed and fired. The bottle was broken into a few big pieces; I put another bottle on the rock and moved back behind him again. He aimed and fired, and this time, the bottle disappeared in many small pieces, meaning his aim was better.

I took another turn. Taki put another bottle and stood aside, but this time a bit closer to the target. I told him to move further away, but he insisted on holding his position. I aimed, pulled the trigger, and saw Taki falling on his back; the bottle disappeared.

Taki was on the ground, screaming, with his hands over his face. I panicked and ran to see where he was hit. I wanted to yell at him about getting too close to the target but concentrated on seeing where he was bleeding from. I noticed that the blood seemed to be coming out of his left cheek. I took my shirt off and wrapped it around his face, trying not to obstruct his nose.

I didn't know what to do as he was still crying from pain. I thought I had better run and find someone to take him to the doctor. I knocked on a few neighborhood doors before someone responded. Luckily, it was *barba* George, and he had a small tractor with a square wooden box attached.

"What? What is it?"

"Barba George, it's my friend. We were doing target practice, and I hit the bottle, and either the glass or the pellets hit him in the face!"

"Where is he?"

"Up on the hill!"

"Get in the box on my tractor, boy. Direct me to him!"

The tractor was very slow, but in a few minutes, we reached Taki. He was still screaming and holding his bandaged face.

We picked him up and placed him in the wooden box, and *barba* George told me to get in there, too, and we were on our way to the doctor. It took us almost half an hour to get there; we picked Taki up and brought him inside the doctor's office, and we were told to wait outside. About half an hour later, the nurse came out to tell us the doctor had removed two pellets lodged in Taki's left cheek.

"He's lucky to be alive," she said sternly. "But he will be all right. You can take him home in an hour."

In the meantime, the bad news traveled fast, and both our mothers, Taki's, and mine, entered the doctor's office in a frenzy, demanding to know what happened and how Taki was doing.

"He's okay!" I hastened to assure them. "He hurt his left cheek, but the doctor treated it and said, 'he can go home in an hour.'"

"Thank God!" Taki's mother cried her eyes toward the heavens.

"But how did it happen?" my mother insisted. "You haven't told us how he got hurt in the first place."

"Well…"

After I finished telling her what and how it happened, she said, "Your father will punish you hard when he hears that you used his shotgun without his permission."

Takis's mother repeated the same words, but they both thanked God that the worst hadn't happened. I knew I was in trouble, but I was ready to take the pain as long as Taki came out without any permanent injuries. We all fell silent, waiting to hear from the doctor when Taki would be able to go home.

Soon after, the doctor's door opened, and this time it was the doctor himself.

"I have removed *three* shotgun pellets," he announced, "and the boy will be okay." We all breathed sighs of relief. "Bring him back in a week to make sure there are no problems. Now come in and help me get the patient to that tractor you've got parked outside my window. Nurse, get us a blanket to line the box with."

Taki seemed depressed; his face was all bandaged up, with a nose-hole for him to breathe through, but he was not in pain, at least until the local anesthesia wore off. He apologized to both mothers and told them he had learned his lesson and would not do such a stupid thing again. We helped him to the tractor and laid him down on the heavy blanket loaned to us by the nurse, and I sat right next to him. We looked at each other, and both shook our heads; then he apologized to me, too, for not listening to me and insisting on standing beside the target.

"You should go home and pray to God that you are still alive," I told him.

I got home to a cold reception from everyone except my father, who was not there yet; I apologized for my actions and said I was exhausted and going to bed. I didn't want to be around to face my father before he had a good sleep. But my mother insisted I should eat something before I went to bed as she knew I must be hungry. Luckily for me, my father didn't get home from *Kafenia* before 12, but the next morning, he was waiting for me to get up. First, he gave me a backhander – a typical step-one punishment: sometimes, it was more than one, depending on the seriousness of the infraction. Then he told me I would never touch his shotgun again. My brother Argiri was also harsh in his reproof.

The main lesson we took out of this venture was a sense of our immaturity and our desire to play with guns because guns were the only toys we had to play with. We thanked God again for saving us from injuries or death one more time.

***

It was early spring, and that brought the seeding of all crops, mainly corn, wheat, potatoes, and other crops, into the food chain. I was told by my brother Argiri to get the plow and all the tools on Truman tomorrow morning; we were going to Vambakies to start plowing several *pezoules* (farm lots) to get them ready for seeding.

Early the next morning, my brother and I had breakfast and got ready to go off to Vambakies. My mother made us our lunch, which consisted of leftovers from our Sunday dinner. This included a few pieces of chicken, half a loaf of *karveli* bread, feta cheese, and olives – the main staples of a farmer's lunch. She put it all in a *sakouli* sack and handed it to me to take with us.

It normally took us 45 minutes to get to the farms on foot and start our daily work. Plowing requires at least two people: one to guide the plow being pulled by the mule, plus one or two others to break up any hard soil and smooth it out so it was ready for seeding.

When we got to the farm, we decided who was going to plow first and which lot to plow, as the farm was divided into different-sized lots, and we had many lots separated by size and some separated by a low stone wall. Because this was my first-year introduction to plowing, my brother took the first turn to plow this rather large lot while I watched and learned how to plow. I wished I was learning a better skill than plowing, but for now, I didn't have that option.

My brother started the plowing, and I followed behind, smoothing the soil with a long, heavy hoe. We made good progress for over two hours. Then, just before we were planning to take a five-minute break, we suddenly heard a loud cracking sound from the tip of the plow under the ground. Truman came to a complete stop, and my brother seemed surprised and disappointed because he feared the plow must have hit a rock and broken the tip. He was hoping it hadn't broken the hard tip because we didn't have a spare one with us today.

After a quick inspection, however, it was clear that this was exactly what had happened: The plow had hit a rock and broken the tip, which is a normal occurrence. When a tip gets broken, and you don't have a spare tip, it means the plowing for the day is over. We were both greatly disappointed about this mishap because we had a limited amount of time to plow all the lots before we could proceed with the seeding.

"Why don't we have a spare tip?" I said. "If we had a spare, we could quickly replace the broken one and continue our plowing instead of having to stop and delay the plowing by two or three days."

"Most years," Argiri replied, "we have at least one spare tip, sometimes even two spare tips, but not this year."

Of course, this was news to me as this was my first year of plowing.

"I'll order two spare tips when I visit the plow shop tomorrow," Argiri said.

We released Truman from the plow straps and allowed him to graze in a different farm lot while we finished a few other tasks before heading back and going to the plow repair shop to order the spares in time for the next day's plowing. Our father was not pleased with what had happened and blamed my brother for not seeing the rock underground; as always, he was quick to lay blame but never to praise. That was my father's response to most of the problems we faced.

We were lucky to get to the two new tips before the repair shop closed, and we were ready for the next day's plowing. This was a typical day of my daily life: no real accomplishments, no hopes and dreams for a better future. But somehow, I managed to escape these desperate thoughts by thinking about what my life was like back when the Nazis were deciding my fate, and that helped me dream of a better future someday. The civil war was now terrorizing our lives and especially the lives of young people, as the guerillas were kidnapping the young and sending them to Albania and other communist countries. My parents decided to send my brother to Athens to attend aircraft mechanic school and keep him from being kidnapped. Now I was left alone to work the farms.

My daily life consisted of walking back and forth to Vambakies, plowing and seeding, and this would continue throughout the spring until midsummer when the seeds became real plants that needed fertilizing and watering. In our area, water was our biggest problem in growing any type of crop. There was public water channeled down to our farms and beyond from reservoirs up north that opened at certain times. Sometimes, it reached us, but most of the time, the water was intercepted by farmers ahead of us while we waited, sometimes through the night, for water that never made it to us.

A few farmers had wells with diesel-run pumps and were able to keep their plants watered, especially during their growing period. We had a well but not a diesel pump, and the only way to get the water out was with what we call a *magani*. More details about the *mangani* in my next chapter.

One day, my father hired his friend to help him cut wood for the winter fireplace and the cooking stove. I was supposed to bring them a cooked meal that my mother made along with some cutting tools, like a well-sharpened axe that my father had forgotten to take with him.

My mother filled up a *Vedoura* (pot) with a handful of baked potatoes in a fresh tomato sauce and made sure the cover was locked so I didn't spill the food. I loaded all the tools my father had asked me to bring, including the freshly sharpened axe; my mother helped me up on the tall donkey, then handed me the pot with the handle, and I was ready to bring lunch to my father and his helper.

"Be careful, Giorgo," she warned me again. "Don't spill anything, but hurry along. Your father will be waiting."

"Don't worry, Mitera, I won't," I said. Then I gave the donkey a gentle nudge to get him moving, and we were off to Vambakies. She waved with another warning to be careful and not to fall off this huge new donkey and spill the warm meal. I didn't want to admit it, but I knew she was worried when I saw the look on her face.

Holding the *Vedoura* with my right hand extended, so I didn't accidentally bump it against the *samari* (saddle), I moved along, up and down the narrow winding road to Vambakies, when suddenly, the donkey went on a kicking spree. Trying to hold on to the *Vedoura*, I lost my balance, and down I went, hitting the ground hard and the *Vedoura* went up in the air. The cover came loose, and all that tasty meal ended up all over my body as I was lying on my back on the hard ground in pain. Little did I know that as I was falling, I had brushed the sharp edge of the axe tied on the back of the *samari*.

I slowly stood up on my trembling feet and felt a sharp pain coming from my left shoulder blade. I quickly started checking my body for cuts and bruises while trying to pinpoint where the pain was coming from. Then I noticed blood flowing down my leg through my short pants and into my shoe. I panicked and started running back home, crying; I couldn't reach the wound in my back to try to stop the bleeding that was flowing into my shoe, making it slippery and harder for me to run fast. Just before I was about to enter the house, I slipped and fell on the ground and let out a loud scream.

Luckily, both my mother and sister were in the house and heard my screams. They came out and saw me on the ground with blood flowing down my left leg, into my shoe, and all over the floor. They helped me inside the house and onto my bed and removed all my clothes, frantically searching for the source of the blood. Having examined the front of my body, they helped me turn over onto my stomach, and my sister let out a scream when she saw blood coming out of a deep and long slice on my left shoulder blade. My mother ran to fetch a clean cloth to try to stop the bleeding.

She placed a thick bandage on the open wound and applied pressure until the bleeding stopped.

"I'm going to clean the wound now, Giorgo," she said by way of a warning. The only antiseptic available in those days was rubbing alcohol, and it was used on all manner of cuts and bruises. "And it's going to hurt."

Yes, it did hurt, but my mother had used this method many times before to clean the many cuts I'd sustained on my body, mostly in my legs from playing soccer, so I knew what to expect, but this time, I knew it was going to be much more painful, and I did brace myself. She then wrapped a clean white cloth around my body and told me to stay in bed for the rest of the day.

When I woke up late in the afternoon, she asked me if I was still in pain, and I couldn't lie to her: I was in pain, so she gave me two aspirins; aspirin was the best painkiller in those days.

"I will make your favorite meal," she said.

My favorite was oven-baked lamb with potatoes, but she said, "We don't have any lamb, just baked potatoes and some avgolemono soup."

I did not complain.

She also told me that the cut was over twelve inches long and almost half an inch deep. Normally, such a cut would have required many stitches at the hospital emergency room, but such luxuries were nonexistent in my village. My wound eventually healed without stitches, and the big scar is visible to this day. When my doctors ask me what happened back here, I always ask if they have the time to hear a donkey story.

After dinner, my mother and I, along with my sister, walked back to where the accident happened to see if the donkey was still around. We found him waiting for us with a sorry-looking face and his *samari* saddle hanging under his belly. In the meantime, my father and his helper never got their meal, and we had no way to tell him what happened until he came home late in the evening, ready to punish me for not bringing lunch and the axe he needed. My mother came to my rescue again, and I avoided another punishment, but he was furious.

Chapter 17:

Life After Nine Years of Horrific

Wars

Freedom at Last

It was hard to believe that I lived through two horrific and destructive wars and survived, unlike many thousands of others who met their deaths by either the inhuman Nazis or the communist *andartes*. I was now a teenager, old enough to pursue my dreams, but they were only dreams. I couldn't see my dreams coming true in Vresthena, which was struggling to rise from the devastation and destruction of two wars – where almost all the houses in the village had been burned down by the Nazis and still lay in ashes, as the villagers had neither the will nor the money to rebuild.

But at least we could now work the fields and prevent starvation, as we had all suffered during the Nazi occupation. We were all working at the farm, waking up early each sunny morning, having breakfast and enjoying a hearty breakfast of eggs with *loukaniko* (sausage), feta cheese, and fresh tomatoes which my mother or sister prepared.

My mother would also prepare lunch for all of us to take to the farm—sometimes leftovers from the night before or sandwiches with my favorite--spam. For dessert, we would have walnuts, figs, boiled chestnuts, and sometimes sweets like *baklava* or *koulurakia*. Then we would be ready for the two-mile walk to the farm behind Truman, the mule.

After that, we had another day of hard work at the farm in Vambakies before us. My father helped to load all our farm tools, including the plow, on Truman.

Spring was one of the busiest seasons for us: preparing the soil for seeding, which meant plowing all the farm lots we planned to seed, each one designated for either corn, potatoes, beans, or wheat.

Truman pulled the plow tilled the soil so that we could seed all our crops. Once the seeds broke through the freshly tilled earth, they needed a lot of water, of which we had very little of, with very few options for irrigation.

Farming in Greece, and especially in our region, was challenging because of the limited amount of good soil for crops; only 20% of our land was farmable for growing crops like wheat, barley, potatoes, tomatoes, corn, and grapes. Our family's farmable land was less than two acres, and our greatest obstacle to achieving a good harvest was the lack of water during the spring and the hot summer growing seasons.

We had three sources of irrigation for our farm. First was the rain, which was the most unreliable source; in some seasons, we didn't have a drop of rain. The second source was water flowing down from the mountains, which was captured by wheat processing mills to turn their large stone wheels and crush the wheat and turn it into white flour, the key ingredient for our main staple, bread. Then this water would flow for more than two miles of *avlakia* (channels). Unfortunately, the ground in our region was highly porous, meaning a lot of precious water seeped into the soil, meaning any farmer along its course could tap into it and water his own farm. Most of the time, the water never reached our farm because it had been used by other farmers upstream from us.

Many nights, I would sleep overnight in the shed, with my brother taking turns, awake under the full moonlight for the water to show up.

Sometimes the water never reached us, other times it did for a short time, but not long enough to water all the crops. Consequently, we could not depend on this source of water.

The third water source was our last resort and most laborious: the well water, but that also was a limited amount of water that had to be extracted via the *mangani,* an old mechanical gadget as shown in the picture below. A mule would trot around the circle, pulling a post tied to the gears that rotated the water buckets, bringing them up full of water, emptying them, and returning them down to the well to refill again until the well was emptied. The entire operation would take more than six hours under the hot summer sun. We would try to water early in the morning before the scorching sun rays made it unbearable for both the mule and the person walking behind, which was one of my jobs.

A Typical Mangani

A few neighboring farmers with deeper wells and faster water streams used gas-driven water pumps that would run for hours and provide enough water for their farms, and sometimes my father would pay a neighboring farmer for the use of his pump to water some of our farm lots that were near his well. He also wanted to use a pump on our well, but it had such a slow water flow, and the pump would empty it in half an hour; then we had to wait twenty-four hours to refill again. So, the pump was not an option with this well, and my father spent money and time digging new holes all over the farm lots, looking for higher water flows. Still, after a dozen holes, some over 20 feet deep, there were no water streams to be found, and finally he gave up looking for better water streams within our farm space. Unfortunately, about half a dozen dry wells were left uncovered. When we had rainstorms, especially up in the mountains, a fast-flowing river would fill up these dry wells that were a danger to humans and animals, who could easily fall in and drown. We lost several goats with their *katsikia* (kid goats) before he could cover these open dry wells and avoid any further tragedies.

During one stormy season, we were full of hope and optimism for a strong crop harvest because of the rain, and our crops were growing green and healthy. The golden corn cobs, the green potatoes, and all our crops were growing unusually healthily, making us highly hopeful of having a successful and robust crop for the first time in many years.

But one early morning, while my brother and I were watering the crops, I suddenly noticed that the bright, hot sunlight was turning dark. My first wishful thought was that it was a raincloud that could trounce us with a heavy rainstorm and water our dying crops. With that wishful thought in my mind and a smile on my face, I looked up at the sky to watch this imaginary black cloud releasing all that water it was holding. Instead, my happy smile turned into fear at the sight of millions of little birds of a kind I had never seen before in my life.

I screamed to my brother, "Look, look! What are those things that are blocking our sun?"

He looked up, and immediately, his calm expression changed to one of horror.

"They are *akrides!*" locusts he said. "Let's run to the shed!"

Looking up at the sky as I ran, I saw a swarm of locusts moving very slowly, blotting out the sun as far as I could see. Suddenly, I looked at my brother, and I noticed that he was covered from head to toe. Then I felt them landing all over me too – these gray, funny-looking creatures, moving up and down our bodies, full of energy and hunger, looking for food. At the same time, we saw our green crops disappearing in front of our eyes.

I panicked and started screaming, afraid of what might happen not just to our crops but to *us*.

I kept crying, "Are they going to eat us alive, too?" I asked my brother as I watched the locusts devouring every inch of our green crops.

My brother grabbed my hand and yelled "let's run" and was half running/half dragging me up the hill towards the shed about a thousand feet away. We kept brushing the locusts off us, but they kept landing on us like heavy snowflakes; however, snowflakes do not make a sound like locusts do when they land on us, nor do they weigh as much. I could hear and feel the weight of hundreds, maybe a thousand, locusts landing on me all the way up the hill until we reached the shed. We tried to brush them all off our bodies before we entered the hut and quickly opened the old wooden door; once inside, we immediately closed it and locked it securely, but still, many remained on us; we also noticed that the wooden window was cracked open and hundreds, maybe thousands of locusts had already entered the shed.

We quickly shut and locked the old and uneven wooden window and tried to kill most of these creatures with a large broom we used to sweep the floor of the shed as they were crawling on the floor and up the stone walls. But many were still limping, but at least we both felt a bit safer inside this old shed my father had built many years earlier to sleep in when we worked late into the night.

"How long will they be around?" I asked my brother.

"I don't know."

I felt my heart sink with his answer.

"But I thought you knew! I thought you had seen them before!" "You recognized them."

He shook his head.

"No, I've never seen them. They've never came this far to our country in my lifetime," he replied with fear in his voice. "But I learned about them in school. They generally migrate from country to country in search of food. Hopefully, they'll fly away again soon."

His answer did not calm my fears a bit.

"Let's wait a while before we open the door," he suggested, and I agreed.

Nervously, I sat down on the blanket again and asked my brother to do the same, but for the first time, I saw sadness all over his face, and it made me worried about what would happen next, but he did sit down on the blanket next to me.

It must have been over an hour or two later when my brother woke me up from a deep sleep.

"I cracked open the door," he said, "and it looks like they've slowed down quite a bit. We should go outside to get a better idea of what's going on."

I was ready, but my back was killing me; the rocks under the old, army blanket had been puncturing my lower back the whole time. I followed my brother as he slowly opened the door and stepped out onto what looked like a thick gray carpet, but it was a thick layer of the dead locusts that had slammed into the shed's stone walls; some were still alive, though moving in slow motion.

We both stood in front of the shed for a moment, reluctant to take our first step onto this "carpet." But we had to make our move eventually, and we heard the crunching sound of locusts under our feet, along with the soft hiss of their struggling wings. It sounded like we were walking on a hot pile of charcoal. As far as the eye could see, it was like God had thrown a humongous gray blanket over everything that used to be green, and there was no sight of Truman and our goats.

My brother kept saying, *"Popo, popo,"* in an agonized murmur: "Wow, wow." I repeated the same expression, only louder. It looked like our entire farm, where all our new green crops used to be that we had worked so hard to grow, had become a cemetery with only a few skeleton corn plants still standing like crosses to mark the graves.

I followed my brother, walking slowly and carefully so as not to slip on the moving ground, which was covered by crawling locusts. We had brought a rope from the shed with us so we could sweep the field clear of locusts, by each holding one end of the rope and swinging it.

Suddenly, I stepped on a layer of locusts that was moving downhill and lost my footing. I let out a scream and fell hard on my back. My brother turned around with a concerned face, asked me if I was all right, and helped me back onto my feet. Luckily, I was unhurt, though I was shaken.

We finally reached the well.

"Go fetch the *sakouli* if it's still there," my brother said.

We had left a *sakouli* full of food hanging on an olive tree near the well. As I approached the olive tree, I could see that the *sakouli* was still hanging there, but it was covered with locusts running in and out of it, and I was afraid there would be no food left. I unhooked the *sakouli* from the branch and shook it up and down to get rid of the locusts. Then I looked inside only to see that it contained nothing but locusts swarming around, still looking for more food.

"Ta Fagone ola," I shouted to my brother. "They ate everything." With that, we returned to the work of clearing the field.

We each grabbed one end of the rope. We started swinging it and walking across the field, trying to dislodge the locusts off any plants that were still standing, a mere fraction of the crop we had worked so hard to grow. They had been healthy yellow-golden corn cobs that would provide *bombota* (cornbread) as well as food for our chickens and hogs; now, the corn had all been eaten by these creatures that came from nowhere to destroy our badly needed crops.

We managed to chase some away, but minutes later, they returned to finish anything edible left standing. We desperately continued swinging the rope, hoping to save some plants. Still, our hope soon turned into desperation and depression. We were helpless; we had lost all our crops, and though we chased the locusts away from one spot, they would simply move to another instead of flying away to another country. It didn't seem they were ready to leave yet.

Now, it was time to find Truman and the two goats. We headed to an area with high and thick olive trees surrounded by tall underbrush; we were hoping that was where Truman and the goats might be. As we got closer, I got a glimpse of Truman's tail swinging back and forth, trying to chase the bugs away; he was under this large olive tree, which was still covered with locusts. I started brushing them off Truman while my brother looked for the goats.

He found one standing among the olive trees, but the other one with its two kids was lying dead on top of the gray carpet, covered by hundreds of locusts, some of whom were going in and out of her open mouth. We were devastated by the loss of our crops and the goat that provided our milk, but we were happy to have found Truman.

It was now getting dark; it was time for us to head home—if we could ever get home—and bury our faces under the bedcovers, and maybe when we woke up in the morning, this day would turn out to be only a nightmare. We walked home, stepping on the same gray carpet for at least half the way; we were more than halfway home when we first stepped on dry ground again.

We returned to find our mother and sister anxiously waiting for us, expecting the worst from this catastrophic event as described by others who had returned.

When I woke up the next day, hoping it was all a nightmare, my mother told me the truth: it was indeed a catastrophic event, and the swarm of locusts had destroyed the entire village's crops, adding to our post-war poverty and hunger.

Wheat Harvesting

Harvesting the wheat was a tremendously laborious job; first, we had to cut the wheat by hand using the *sikale*, then we bundled the sheaves into small bales and tied them with a rope, making it easy to load them on the mule and transport them to the *aloni* to be stamped by horses to separate the chaff.

It was an ancient method: one or several mules, horses, or donkeys galloped around a flat stone *aloni* loaded with many bales of wheat, mashing the wheat underfoot until the bales were reduced to a mixture of chaff and grain.

The aloni, separating the grain from the chaff.

This process would take the entire day – maybe two, depending on the volume of wheat bales and the number of horses. After the wheat bales had been cut up into small pieces, the final separation of the grain from the chaff began. That process is called winnowing – we would toss the mixture of grain and chaff up in the air in light wind, which would gradually blow the chaff away, whereas the grain would fall straight down into the *aloni*. This was a very laborious process that relied on the wind being slight but steady, and depending on the cooperation of the elements, the entire process might take a week or two. We used to sleep on the *aloni* so that we could take full advantage of the best wind as long as it lasted; we would keep winnowing throughout, and at times, we would take turns to sleep for a few hours while others kept on winnowing as long as the wind blew.

Some of the Other Annual Key Harvests

Grape Harvest

This was my favorite harvest after the dusty and hard work of wheat harvesting because I loved to eat sweet white grapes, a reward for helping my father to grow and keep animals like foxes and blackbirds from having wild parties, eating and destroying our vines, and running around looking for the best grapes to eat or peck on. Unlike our other complicated and laborious harvests, this was like a festival, maybe because everyone picking grapes couldn't help but consume more than they should have, which made them feel merry. The grape harvest started in the fall and lasted almost a week, depending on the weather. After all the grapes were cut, we carried them on our backs or on donkeys in these large woven baskets and carried them to the stomping tank inside the *catoi* (basement).

236

This was my favorite harvest as I took my turn to stomp the grapes and scrape the wine barrels before we poured in the Musto. Musto is the grape juice after adding the yeast so that it can turn the concoction into wine in the barrel.

Olives Harvesting

Picking olives from the trees was laborious work that started in late fall when the weather was always cool and sometimes freezing. The pickers would climb a ladder propped against the inside of an olive tree, grab each branch full of olives and dragged the olives off the branch and drop them into a bag hanging from their waists. All the work was done by hand, and by the end of the day, the hands would be full of blisters.

The olives had to be ripe and blue before they could be harvested. My grandfather had planted many olive trees on every piece of land he owned, spread out all over the area, and some were as far as one or two hours apart; it took time to reach them, and we had to travel back and forth many times, carrying the olives home in large sacks and, finally, to the *litrivio*, the olive-processing mill, which turned the olives into pure virgin olive oil for our family consumption; we sold any surplus.

The *litrivio* was located near the village center and was powered by steam, which was generated by a vast wood-burning chamber that ran the engines and rotated the two colossal stone wheels, which rolled around in an enclosed stainless steel olive container; they crushed the olives as they rolled, and the olive oil drained into a large bronze container. The oil was then delivered to our homes in goatskin sacks and emptied into our large ceramic storage containers, ready for our family's consumption until the next year's harvest.

Picking Olives

Typical olive-crushing stone wheel.

This process would normally take a day or two, depending on the volume of olives to be processed, and before our olives were processed.

The day our olives were processed, I was standing in front of that huge tank watching these two giant stone wheels rolling around inside this stainless-steel tank crushing the olives and the olive oil pouring into a storage tank—a fascinating experience for a young boy watching how our tasty olive oil was generated.

Honey Harvest

My father had about a dozen beehives near the shed that overlooked our farm. This hive accomplished two major functions. First, the bees generated all the honey for our family's consumption, and we sold any surplus. Secondly, the bees pollinated our crops for better yields.

These are two and three beehives stacked.

A beehive is a rectangular wooden box in which the honeybees live and produce the honey we all love eating over the thick Greek yogurt – my favorite – or spread over toasted bread or all those Greek sweets (*glyka*) my mother used to make.

Bees are some of the most precious little creatures on our planet, although more commonly seen as nuisances by many people that mistake them as wasps. National Geographic estimates that one in every three bites a person eats is from a bee-pollinated nut or flower.

The size of a single hive is 16x 22" and contains ten frames with a densely packed group of hexagonal cells made of beeswax, called a honeycomb. The bees use the cells to store food, honey, and pollen. The hives are stackable, and you can add up to four units, but you don't want the wind to blow them down, so most of ours were one or two, not higher.

When I was younger, I used to watch from a distance as my father harvested the honey from a distance because I was afraid of being stung by the bees. I was stung once, and I knew very well the sting and swelling that lasted for a day or two. Now that I was older, my father asked me to help him when it was time to harvest. The best time, he said, was late summer, when bees had a chance to fill and cap all the cells in each frame. Now he asked me to help him harvest the honey, as he was getting tired of doing it.

When it was time to harvest, we both wore protective gear and approached the hive with a smoker; the smoke calms the bees and makes them less aggressive while we take their honey away.

The Smoker

The extractor, we had to remove the thin wax cap on top of the cells so the honey could easily flow out into a large pan as we rotated the extractor.

A Typical Honey Extraction

The honey frames are placed in the tank vertically. With the handle, we rotate the frames inside the tank, and the honey is sucked out by the centrifugal force—another fascinating procedure.

Walnut Harvesting (The last harvest of the year)

In late fall, another annual task we had to do was harvesting walnuts, a key ingredient in many of our daily diets and in many dishes and sweets. We had several walnut trees, some very large, which we had to physically climb with tall ladders and bang each tree branch with a long and robust stick specially trimmed from small, straight maple trees found in the forest. If they survived through the end of the walnut harvest, we kept them for the next year. We moved up the tree branch by branch and knocked down every ripe walnut that we could see and reach. After checking to make sure we got all the walnuts from the tree, it was time to pick them up.

They were lying all over the ground, and some had fallen into thorny bushes, and we tried to retrieve as many as we could but did not spend a lot of time dealing with these thorny bushes; we left those walnuts for the hungry critters. With smaller walnut trees, we could reach all the branches from the ground and didn't have to climb them. After picking them from the ground, we carried them home in large sacks my mother had woven. In most seasons, we harvested more than we could consume. I took the surplus walnuts to Sparta, sold them in the food market, and kept half of the profits.

When we had completed the annual harvest, we stored all the commodities like wheat, corn, potatoes, olive oil, wine, honey, and walnuts in the wooden storage bins in our storage room.

The Death of My Grandfather

During our chaotic daily life – we had to finish the harvest while our country was mired in civil war – more bad news came to our family. My grandfather, George Kaperonis, my mother's father, died after many years of bedridden illness. I have many good memories of my grandfather. There was the time I first stayed with him overnight in his little house next to his *mandri* goathouse, and we sat together in front of a wood-burning fireplace, eating chestnuts we had roasted on hot charcoal. My grandfather placed the chestnuts on the charcoal with a long, wooden fork-like stick while telling me his overwhelming life stories. Stories of him as a soldier fighting the Ottoman Turks in the early 1900s and then the Germans in WWI – history I had not learned despite growing up under the Nazis. I could visualize him fighting in similar battles that I had witnessed, and I understood and believed his stories. This was a special, unforgettable time in my life spent with my grandfather that I will never forget

I will also never forget another moment with my grandfather before he died. I vividly remember him lying in his bed with his head propped up so he could talk to our village attorney, dictating his testament with a low and faint voice that made it hard to comprehend his words. The attorney had to move his ear next to my grandfather's mouth to hear and understand his wishes. He willed all his assets to his daughter, my mother, Panagiota Kakridas, to distribute as she wished, with only one exception: that his house be willed to me, George Kakridas, his grandson. How can I forget such a gift?

His death came almost three years after my grandmother, Vasilo, his wife, had died. After that painful event, I watched my mother sobbing while her mother was lowered into the open grave, and today, I would be witnessing another sad family loss – my grandfather, with all my many great memories of growing up with him before and during the Nazi occupation, keeping our family alive with milk, cheeses, and other food products.

After the church service, we all followed his coffin, with the priest leading the procession to the cemetery. This was my second time entering this dreadful place since my grandmother's death over three years earlier, yet it seemed like it was yesterday. My mother was very close with her father, and she cared for him for over five years as he suffered from an indescribable medical condition. She expected all of us to show the same

244

devotion and support in both physical and mental assistance as he was suffering from some undiagnosed ailment, and we all unconditionally did.

And now she was ready to bury him, and I was standing next to her as I was at her mother's burial, sad and depressed. The burial service in our Greek Orthodox religion is long and painful. She had been sobbing for hours, and now it was time to lower him into his grave as they did with my grandmother. This time, she screamed louder than I had ever heard; she almost fainted, and if my father hadn't been there to hold her, she might have fallen into the grave herself.

A few days later, after she had recovered from her father's burial, she reminded us that it was time to resolve another gruesome matter required by Greek law: to exhume her mother's remains, and she asked my father to arrange it soon.

"It's been a bit over three years, and we don't want to be fined," she said.

For me, it had been an agonizing unanswered question since my mother had mentioned it to me earlier. This was not a good time to ask her, but I was only ten years old, and I thought I should know the answer to this gruesome and degrading fact of human life after death.

"Why must we exhume dead people's remains?" I said. "And what happens to them after they are exhumed?"

"Sit here next to me."

I did, and she placed her right hand behind my head and caressed it while she answered my question.

"To your first question: It is Greek law that three years after a person is buried, they must be exhumed."

"But *why?*"

"I'm coming to that. Why? In order to make room for others. The exhumed remains are placed in a wooden box with their name and dates of birth and death on it, and that box is kept in a little gated house at the corner of the cemetery so their loved ones can go and visit them—if the annual maintenance fee is paid."

"Why not make the cemetery larger? Or build another cemetery? We have so much land all around us."

To me, this childish demand still seems to be a reasonable question, but it was one to which my mother had no answer.

Many years later, after my mother had passed, I visited the cemetery to see where my mother's bones were resting. I found them in a square box with her name on it: "Panagiota Kakridas." I stood there for a few minutes, staring at the box containing my mother's bones.

Chapter 18:
Applied for My Visa

Another war was now over, except this one was more devastating and more divisive because it was between the same people, the same country, the same religion, and the same culture.

It was brother against brother, father against family, and neighbor against neighbor. We were not fighting a foreign culture; it was Greeks against Greeks.

This was a long, murderous, and shameful war that was rooted in the last war. After five years of occupation, the loss of freedom and pride in our heritage and love for our country, this war drove us to turn our hate on each other instead of on our real enemy.

America helped Greece to defeat the communists and prevented the country from falling into the hands of the Soviet Union and becoming part of the Communist Bloc like our neighbors to the north and other countries that fell under communist regimes after World War II.

Greece was free again, and the government forged ahead with rebuilding its shattered economy and its infrastructure, which was devastated by the Nazis and the civil war. Now, to most young people my age, the future looked bleak. There were no jobs in Greece, and we began to emigrate to other countries like Canada, Australia, and Germany for the chance of work and a better life. This was a huge sacrifice; most of us left our loved ones behind and, in many cases, never returned to Greece.

America had been our savior in both wars and knew very well the problems we faced in generating jobs for people, especially our younger generation. Now, America came to the rescue again by opening its doors to Greeks that could qualify for this generous new program.

The program was called *"Antartopliktous"* for people afflicted by the civil war. To qualify for the program, you had to provide proof that you were afflicted with personal and family suffering created by the civil war and provide sponsorship papers from a US citizen/relative guaranteeing that they would care for all your needs so that you would, in no way, be a burden to American taxpayers.

These American leaders cared about protecting the American taxpayer, unlike today's corrupt leaders that allow people to enter illegally and then go directly to social programs that were put in place for American citizens and abuse and disrespect American laws and the American way of life. That was the core requirement to qualify for this program. I was among the lucky people who qualified for this generous gift from the American Government and its generous people.

My mother lost no time in writing to her brother, my godfather, Gus, with a copy of the immigration requirements, asking him to hurry and send the necessary papers to Athens.

Within a couple of weeks, we received a letter from the immigration office confirming the receipt of my sponsorship papers, and I was directed to report to the immigration office within two weeks. My mother hugged me and broke down in tears; it was a dream come true for her to see me go to America, though we both knew it was only the beginning of a long and difficult process of getting a visa and passport.

My first trip to Athens in 1950 to apply for this program was my first step toward civilization after witnessing the devastation of two wars. It was like a dream to me. My mother accompanied me, riding the bus from the village to Sparta and then taking the bus to Athens. She was more excited for me than I was for my having this golden opportunity and, hopefully, becoming an American citizen and having the chance to live the American dream.

My mother realized that the price she had to pay was for me to leave her and the likelihood that I might never return. This was a painful realization, but she was willing to endure it to see me have a better life. She witnessed my day-to-day desperation of living without hope and dreams. Now she was excited to give me hope for a better life. She already knew the consequences of both options, and she chose the one that gave me a chance to leave this miserable life for a better one. I can never forget her sacrifices to accomplish that.

As the time for me to board the bus in Sparta approached, my mother hugged me and kissed me and wished me good luck in my first step toward achieving my lifelong dream of going to America. I can never forget that first trip.

The bus driver made sure that everyone was on board and seated; there were no seat belts then. He started the bus's loud diesel engine and began moving through the streets of Sparta. I looked behind to see my mother, with tears on her face, still waving at me. The bus driver told us

249

that our next stop would be Tripoli, which I learned in school is the capital of the State of Arcadia.

The bus crossed the Evrota river bridge and went on to the winding one-lane road to Athens. My heart pounded like it wanted to jump out of my chest. This was a very exciting time for me.

The driver was in his mid-forties and seemed to be a serious and careful driver as he navigated those winding and narrow roads, regularly looking in his rear mirror to see if another bus or any other vehicle was trying to pass him; it was a one-lane road, and there was no passing allowed unless there was an emergency, in which case buses had to pull over on the roadside and allow the emergency vehicle to pass.

We drove by this stretch of the road named Monodendri, (the same infamous place where the Nazis murdered 118 innocent people) and where we could see my village. In fact, I could see our house because it was the last house in the village and below the *alataria*, the same small hill where my friends and I played soccer and other dangerous games. This was the spot of the road very visible from our village and especially from our terrace, where I used to watch the German truck convoys heading toward Sparta and to our village.

The bus reached the city of Tripoli about two hours later. The driver parked the bus near a café so we could take half an hour to rest and have something to eat. After our rest and a fresh cup of Greek coffee with *koulurakia* (Greek cookies), we boarded the bus and headed to Athens; we had another six-hour trip ahead of us.

We drove through many small villages and towns like Tripoli and Argos. Argos was one of the towns I had read about in school but never

dreamed of ever going there. This was the first and longest bus trip I had ever taken. I was getting a bit tired, but I was still very excited to see new towns with many people and cars on the streets, and I enjoyed the scenery along the way.

As the bus was speeding down the road, my mind traveled back to the dark days of the Nazi occupation and then to the civil war; but then, I would snap back to reality every time the bus slowed down and stopped to drop off or pick up new passengers.

After we passed through Tripoli, a town the size of Sparta, we came to a famous stretch of road that everyone, who passed through before me, talked about--- how the bus would seem to disappear from the peak of the road as it dipped about ten meters, then rose back up again, repeating this sensation for about a mile. I had never been on an airplane, but those who had told me this sensation was like what you felt on an airplane. The bus ride through this stretch of road was a memorable one and felt as real as I'd been told.

My next biggest surprise was seeing, for the first time in my life, the awesome sight of the ocean. Although I had seen pictures of an ocean in my geography class in school, I will never forget this beautiful, majestic view—an endless body of blue water called the Aegean Sea. I was so excited to see this vast amount of water; it seemed like there was no end in sight except for a few boats that looked like they were standing still. It was hard for me to believe that, as far as I could see, there was nothing but clear blue water.

Then the bus entered another famous road that wound down from the top of the mountain. The danger and fear of the possibility that a bus

or a car could tumble over 500 feet to the bottom of the mountain in case of an accident or by simply missing or not navigating a turn carefully and precisely made this road a must that everyone who traveled to Athens had to experience.

At some point on the road, there was not enough room for two vehicles to pass, especially large trucks and buses. Both had to stop on the edge of the road and slowly and carefully make the pass. This part of the road to Athens was then called the *Colosurti*, and everyone traveling to Athens had to go through this dangerous portion where the bus would travel down a steep winding road to the bottom of the mountain.

Our bus started at the top of the mountain and slowly drove down through the dangerous narrow road while all the passengers on the bus stared straight ahead and dared not look towards the bottom of the mountain because it was very scary. We watched the driver move slowly and carefully, because one miscalculation of his speed in the turns could send us rolling down the bottom of the mountain.

After twenty minutes on our ride down the winding one-lane road that seemed endless, we finally reached the bottom safely. With a big sigh of relief and loud applause for the driver, we continued on the road to Athens.

About eight long hours from Sparta, we arrived in Athens, where my brother was waiting to pick me up. He drove me to his house for dinner and for a badly needed rest after my long bus ride.

The next day, he took me to the immigration office to start my papers process, but I had no idea what I was in for. I spent the first day waiting in long lines. By the end of the day, I was told the office was

closing for the day and to come back the next day—my first of many more disappointments to come.

Many days later, after dealing with the Greek bureaucracy, I was told to come back the next week with certain personal certificates that had to be done in Sparta, so I left for home. After a week of battling with the village bureaucrats to attain the required certificates, I returned to Athens. This time, the trip was not as exciting as my first one; in fact, it was boring and extremely tiring.

Almost six months had gone by, and I was not any closer to getting my passport. Now, there were rumors that the immigration quota would come to a close. People were getting nervous and exhausted from standing in long lines for hours and sometimes for days, dealing with the rudest, most unprofessional, and most ignorant office clerks of the Greek immigration office.

When I went back the next day and stood in the back of the same old line, we were told that those who had not reached a certain level in the process, and I was one of those people, had to go back home; we would be notified by letter. This was astoundingly bad news for everyone, but especially for me because I had high expectations of walking the streets of America soon. Looking around me, I saw and heard many people sobbing loudly. All of us standing in line started crying and sobbing, too. It was a sad sight—like we had all lost a mother or a brother.

I took the bus back to the village, and I remember crying on the way home as I realized I had lost my chance to live my dream.

A week later, I received an official letter telling me that this program had filled its quotas but that they would be offering a new

program in a few years. I cried again for missing a lifetime opportunity. I started to blame my father! He was not diligent in rushing to get the papers requested by immigration; he never took anything with a serious intent of finishing with urgency. I slowly accepted my fate and started counting the days, months, and years waiting for the next quota program.

In the meantime, I settled down and continued my day-to-day hopeless life, working at the farm, walking around the *pigadi* (well), behind Truman, bringing the water out of the well to water the corn and potatoes—plants that would stop growing and most likely die without the well water—but I never stopped dreaming of a second chance to go to America.

It was the middle of 1953; there was still no word about a new *Antartopliktous* program, and I was extremely depressed, just waiting. Every afternoon, I asked the mailman, Fotis, if he had any letters for me. Because everyone in the village knew of my situation, including the mailman who was my father's best friend, he wouldn't have to say anything. He just shook his head, and I knew there was no letter for me. The following day, I went back to the *horafia* with my friend Truman, the mule, to water the potatoes from the *pigadi*.

A couple of days later, we took my little brother with us to keep an eye on him because he always got in some kind of trouble, like falling off the terrace or on rocks.

It was a beautiful but hot spring day, and I was plowing the land with Truman to get it ready for the corn and potatoes we would plant. My father and mother were behind me, smoothing out the plowed earth with picks and other farming tools.

A few hours later, we all stopped to eat the lunch my mother had cooked the night before, and we called my little brother, Mitso (his nickname), to come and eat with us as he was wandering around the farm looking for trouble.

After we finished our tasty lunch and washed it down with our own home-brewed retsina wine, my father was getting ready to leave for the *platia,* as was his usual routine. My mother and I continued plowing, and Mitso headed up toward the shed near the beehives; we thought he might want to go to sleep in the shed, so we continued working.

Then we were interrupted by screams coming from the beehive area. I looked up and saw Mitso standing in front of a beehive where the busy bees were coming and going like a busy highway; some were coming to unload their collected nectar, and others were going out to collect nectar from the flowers around the farm. He was screaming and waving his hands, trying to brush off the mad bees from stinging him. I stopped Truman from plowing and ran back to the shed to get my protective gear because I didn't want to get stung, and by the time I got there, Mitso was covered by hundreds of mad bees all over his exposed body—legs, arms, and face. I tried to brush off some of the bees before I picked him up and carried him away to a safe place.

I put him down on the ground and brushed off the rest of the bees from all over his body, and my mother arrived with a bottle of vinegar, screaming and yelling at him while he was also screaming; I had two screamers on my hands. She washed all over his body with vinegar, as that is the best antidote for bee stings. Unfortunately for the bees, they die after the sting, but I had no time to worry about the bees at that time.

Mitso's face was now so swollen that his eyes were completely shut; he looked like a boxer off the ropes after 15 rounds, but he was still screaming his lungs out. Then he went into shock. We quickly broke down the plowing equipment, gathered our belongings, and the goat and her two little ones, put Mitso on Truman, and tied him down -- he was still crying.

We finally got home, and my mother removed all his clothes and washed his whole body with vinegar again and put him to bed and covered him up with a heavy blanket as he now had the chills, but he finally went to sleep, and the crying stopped. The next day the swelling was down, and he was able to slightly open one eye. It took a couple of days for him to get back on his feet since most of the swelling had gone, and he was ready for another adventure.

Hunting

Hunting was not only my favorite sport; it was also part of our food supply. There were no butcher shops in town to buy our meat. We raised chickens, pigs, *kounelia* (rabbits), sheep, and goats, so we could add meat to our dinner table. My father by this time allowed me to use his shotgun to go hunting with my hunting buddies with hunting dogs or moon hunting after the sun went down. If we had a full moon, we would go to certain areas where we had already found rabbit droppings, so we knew they fed there at night.

We would find the right spot in an open field sitting comfortably behind bushes or up on a tree branch where we had 360-degree visibility of the kill zone; the moonlight was not obstructed by a tree or a branch. We could easily see the rabbits coming into the killing zone. It was a quiet, tranquil, and enjoyable moonlit evening; we listened to the night sounds

256

of crickets until a rabbit showed up. Then the tranquility turned into a war zone, and one or two rabbits ended up on our kitchen table.

One of my hunting friends gave me a puppy from a family of hunting dogs. I named her Spitha, which means "quick mover," because I wanted to believe she was one. I took her with me on a real hunting trip with real hunting dogs, hoping she could pick up a few hunting tips. I wasn't too impressed the first time I took her, but I was not ready to give up yet.

On another day after heavy rain—the best time to go hunting since animals are hungry and eager to get out of their hiding places and find something to eat—after a hard day's work, I took my father's double-barreled shotgun and a few shells. I went to my grandfather's *mantri* (goat house) and I sat down under a *karidia* (walnut tree) on a pile of rocks and waited for rabbits to come out of the woods. The hot sun was finally going down, and I sat there alone and waited for about an hour listening to the birds singing and watching them flying around from tree to tree as they, too, were looking for food, and between the birds singing and working all day, I caught myself snoozing a couple of times, and now the sun had gone behind the tall mountain in front of me, and it was starting to get a bit dark.

This time, I was snoozing, but I was startled by a loud jumping sound. When I opened my eyes, I was staring at a rather large rabbit that was staring back at me with his large eyes and large ears, trying to figure out if I was a danger to him and start running fast or ignore me and start chomping green grass. He was standing about 50 feet away from me, and for a second, I thought I was dreaming, but then I realized I was awake and looking at the guy I had come about three miles to find. Then I slowly brought my shotgun up to my sight, and after a few seconds, I pulled the trigger. This was my first kill; I was excited, and I felt good to be able to bring home food for our family. I walked home about two miles, singing and carrying the rabbit and gun on my back. I couldn't wait until I got home to show my mother that our next few meals were on me, and I knew she would be proud of me.

Another time, three of us were using hunting dogs. We usually took a position where we thought the rabbit would travel. We waited, listening to the dog's barking to signal us. When they were close to a rabbit's hiding spot, they would bark loud and fast, and we knew they were chasing one. I walked slowly and carefully toward the dog barking in the woods, and when I got there, I was looking at three dogs trying to hold down what seemed to be a wolf. I tried to aim, but the dogs were coming into my gunsight.

I finally got a kill shot and pulled the trigger. The wolf was dead. Afterward, I was happy that I was able to take a clear shot at the wolf without hurting any of the dogs. I considered it a small miracle and maybe good shooting. Who knows? I was too young and inexperienced a hunter to pat myself on the back for good shooting, but I did anyway.

My friends helped me carry the wolf home, where my father skinned him and sold the skin, as it was valuable at the time for making heavy winter coats. I got my share of several drachmas.

It was now 1954, and there were rumors in the newspaper that America was getting ready to bring another group of Antartopliktous to America. I kept my ears and eyes open. After work, I used to go to the *platia* like most of my friends.

I used to wear American clothes from Uncle Gus. I combed my hair straight back with a part in the middle, as that was the fad at the time. Since hairspray was non-existent then, I used to pour some sugar into my palms, mix it with water, and smooth it over my hair with my hands. It worked like cement, and the girls liked it, but they wouldn't dare talk to me in the *platia* because it was forbidden by village rules.

My friends and I: Dino, Fotis, and Peter

Walking up and down the platia with Peter Viris and Dino Tingos, the son of the mailman, Fotis Tingos, my friends and I checked out the young girls as they were shopping or just walking through the *platia*, probably checking out the boys, too. We wouldn't dare stop a girl to talk in the *platia* in front of others unless they were our sisters or cousins. The rules were very strict and archaic, and we followed them or else! If we wanted to meet a girl in an isolated place and mostly under cover of darkness, secret signals were used. Later, Peter and I were seeing two sisters under the cover of darkness until we all went to America to different cities.

My primary mission was to wait for the mailman, *Barba* Foti (Uncle Foti), to deliver the mail in case he, hopefully, had the letter I had been waiting on for almost four years. He was like Santa Claus to me who would be bringing me a present I was waiting for. If he missed someone, he looked for and found every letter's recipient through the streets, the *tavernas*, and *kafenia*. And he would find him the next evening or until their mail was hand-delivered. He was also a very tall, polite, and pleasant man, respected by all residents. He was my father's good friend; they hunted together.

Chapter 19:
My Village

Vresthena was one of the villages which were part of the municipality called Oinountas, first established in 1835. Vamvakou, then Vresthena, was included in 1840. Then it was abolished in 1912, and the municipality was split into the independent communities of Vamvakou, Vresthena, Vasaras, and Arachova.

At an altitude of 800 meters, Vresthena, my birthplace, is sandwiched between two tall, majestic mountains. These mountains which surround the village made one feel that the Greek gods wanted to protect this beautiful village from all enemies, natural or human.

Vresthena is located on a grassy green hillside dotting the ground with white stone houses and beautiful red-tile roofs, visible from far away.

This is a summer photo of Vresthena with our beautiful Byzantine church; the second image is a view of the village from our house:

Vresthena in the Summer

Vresthena in the Winter

The abundance of trees in our village ranged from pines, walnuts, olives, and a lot of fruit trees, like figs, pears, and peaches, as well as winemaking grapes. The eating grapes were usually found hanging over the terraces and gardens next to every house where a lot of our fresh daily vegetables were grown.

The journey from Sparta to the village is an enjoyable one: driving down a beautiful scenic road lined with olive trees, grapevines, and small, white-painted houses with chickens, dogs, and pigs looking for food and running around the green gardens, and shepherds tending their herds, grazing on the grassy hills and valleys.

When a herd of goats or sheep needs to cross the dusty road, they do not stop and wait for the traffic to slow down; the traffic stops for them. Buses and cars must come to a complete stop to let the herd of goats and sheep, guided by the sheepdogs, cross safely. This sight is always a beautiful moment to enjoy—seeing the animals treat the manmade roads as just another piece of land that belongs to them.

The road to Vresthena splits off the main paved highway from Sparta to Athens, and all the way to the village was an unpaved, dusty road full of potholes until it was finally paved in later years.

At its peak between 1936 and 1950, the village population was estimated to be between 1,000 and 1,500 permanent residents who made their living by plowing the fields and planting wheat, potatoes, corn, and other vegetables that were necessary to feed their families.

Later, after the Greek civil war, most of the young working people migrated to other large Greek cities, Europe, the US, Canada, and Australia looking for work and a better life, and the number of full-time residents was reduced to around fifty or fewer during the winters and approximately three hundred during the summers.

Vresthena had one general store, located in the center of the village owned by Sarantos Karigianis, three Greek cafés (*kafenia*) where patrons drank coffee and played cards (*kolitsina*), several *tavernas* that served *retsina* wine and *mezedes audorves*, and one post office run by Fotis Tingos, a well-liked civil servant and a very close friend of my father's. Everyone called him Foti; he hand-delivered the mail to all residents that happened to be in the *platia* each evening by 6 PM, rain or shine.

There was also a well-built grade school with six large classrooms and a playground, where we took out our classroom frustrations by playing soccer—now with real balls.

Our beautiful Greek Orthodox church built of marble in the Byzantine style was the center of our faith and a marvel to the surrounding villages; everyone who came and stood before this beautiful building felt the power of their Orthodox faith.

Our Greek Orthodox Church

The church was a key part of our way of life. Every Sunday, our mother would dress us up to go to the service.

The History of Our Church

It was every villager's dream to build a grand church where everyone could pray, hear the divine liturgy, and enjoy their Sundays and all holidays.

The people's dream of building a church was beginning to become a reality when the funds were secured by immigrants from Vresthena living abroad, and in 1902, the construction of this magnificent Byzantine architectural design began. Its foundation was soft, so it was filled with trunks of chestnut trees to harden and stabilize it. The entire village went to work to build their dream church. They brought the marble from a nearby quarry on mules and donkeys. The young men and schoolboys worked intensely to bring the sand from our river, about four miles away, through dense, oak-forested hills and rocky, narrow, winding paths on donkeys.

The church took over 14 years to complete and was inaugurated in 1916 and dedicated to the birth of the Virgin Mary. The anniversary is celebrated every year on August 8, which is the biggest annual festival. The entire village and hundreds, sometimes thousands, come from all over Greece and many other countries like America, Canada, and Australia to visit the church.

The celebration usually lasts for three days of eating roast lamb and drinking homemade *retsina* wine, and dancing through the night. This is one festival that no one wanted to miss.

At the main entrance of the church there is a side door which leads to the marbled second floor. From there, one has a panoramic view of the entire congregation. The interior church walls below are adorned with beautiful and colorful icons of various saints and Jesus with his twelve disciples in the center, a joyous and unforgettable religious experience in our young lives.

The church has two entrances; the west side is the main entrance, symbolizing the worshippers entering from the darkness of sin into the light of the truth. Immediately to the right is the *pango* (stand), filled with candles and a tray for parishioners to deposit their contributions to the church. It is protocol to light a candle and place it in the sandbox next to the *Panagia* (Blessed Mother of God) icon, followed by doing your *stavro* (cross), saying a prayer, and kissing the icon.

The Church's Main Entrance

On each side of the sanctuary (*iero*) are the two-chanter *psalteria*, gated stands with a door for the chanters.

We had one great chanter, Kostas Bouzis, who filled the church with his religious melodies and hymns that made all the parishioners inside the church feel closer to God.

Later, when I was around 13 years old, I always stood next to the chanter stand and chanted along with the chanter, Mr. Bouzis. Then one day, he asked me if I wanted to join him and be his assistant. I felt very proud, but shy, to be asked to do such a job, and reluctantly, I joined him the following Sunday. He allowed me to read from certain verses for several Sundays until I realized that this was not my calling, so I went back to my old position and continued to chant next to him.

During the Christmas holidays, we used to walk up the stairs to the second floor with our lit candles to observe the liturgy and chant the Christmas hymns. This filled our hearts with love and belief in Jesus Christ, and we enjoyed the panoramic view of the entire congregation.

My father was a church council member for many years, and he used to take us all to church every Sunday, where I also had my duties as an altar boy.

Christmas was a very special time for all the kids my age because, on Christmas morning, we used to go around to each house in our village and sing hymns called *calandra*.

First, we would knock on the door and ask, "*Na ta poume?*" (Can we sing? If the answer was "*na ta pite*" (yes), we started singing, and when we finished, the door would open, and we would be greeted with a smiling face and a wish of "Merry Christmas". A hand usually came forward with a present. Most of the people gave us fruit, like an orange or a few chestnuts, or candy (*karameles*), and some gave us money, a few *drachmas*.

We were done by noontime; then we returned home and shared our presents with our siblings. Usually, that was our Christmas present; there were not many nicely wrapped presents with bows under the Christmas tree like most kids around the world were used to having. But one Christmas, my mother gave me one present in a paper bag. It was a small, bright red plastic airplane with a small propeller on the front, but I was devastated because when I pulled it out of the bag, I broke the tiny propeller—but my mother said, "Don't worry, Giorgo, your father will fix it".

I was so happy I hugged and kissed my mother for this great present. I kept it next to my bed, just looking at it, but my sister tried to make it fly by throwing it across the room. I was afraid she would break it completely, so I hid it so she couldn't find it anymore. I was afraid she wanted to destroy it because she was jealous that I got a present and she didn't.

At the edge of the *platia*, there is a famous water fountain with four lion heads continuously dispensing fresh, clear, cold water piped down from the *kefalari* originating from deep inside the mountain. To be photographed drinking fresh cold water from this famous lion's mouth fountain is at the top of every visitor's list of things to do when they visit Vresthena.

Next to the water fountain are two tall, old maple trees famous for their longevity and resiliency. Over the past 150 years, they have stood the test of many catastrophic storms as well as occupations and wars.

A Four-Lion Head Water Fountain

On the top left of the church is the bell tower that was added after the church was built with money donated by people who had emigrated to America and other countries.

The church bells ring for various religious purposes: when church starts and also three times a day: at 6 AM, 12 noon, 6 PM, and during funeral processions. The time every hour could be heard more than fifty miles away and helped the farmers, shepherds, and people that didn't have watches keep the time of day. And it rang when the Germans were coming.

The village was built half on a valley and half on a hill that stretched all the way up to the *alataria* where our house was and close to the *kefalari*, freshwater storage.

The Dexameni Water Storage

The *dexameni* (water storage) had a locked steel entry door on the top upper section with a steel ladder going down to the bottom, so workers could perform maintenance when needed, and two windows on the right side near the steps for visual inspection of the water levels. During the Nazi occupation, we watched the naked German soldiers swimming in our drinking water storage which enraged the villagers.

Next to the *dexameni* is a little chapel of *Agios Gianis*, (St. John), where we had many festivities, like baptisms and other family events. Sometimes, the top of the *dexameni* was used for the wedding festivities. The water stored in the *dexameni* was the main source of drinking water and watering our gardens. It was channeled throughout the village via narrow cement canals (*avlakia*) to water our gardens, but the drinking

271

water was piped to the neighborhood centers. People had to bring tin cans to put the water in—hard work that my siblings and I had to do a few times a day for the family's drinking and cooking needs.

Vresthena is the greenest village of all the surrounding villages like Vambakou, Arahova, Vasara, and Varvitsia, and the reason for all that beautiful greenery in the village was the abundance of fresh water.

Going to our *horafia* farms every day was a torturous, tiring walk for us as well as for our animals. We walked through narrow, rocky paths down the hill to the river, then walked about a mile up the river when it was dry to our farms.

The river, which runs north to south, is not active during the summer months. It becomes dangerous and impassible only after a heavy storm, when it carries heavy logs, trees, and sometimes dead animals, forcing us to wait, sometimes a day or more, to be able to reach our *horafia*.

The River Originates from Surrounding Mountains

This river flows only after heavy rainstorms. It gains strength as it flows south from the surrounding mountain streams, causing serious damage to our fields adjacent to the river. It eventually falls into the Evrota river in Sparta.

Chapter 20:
Going to America

I had been dreaming of going to America to try and heal all the wounds in my body and soul caused by nine years of living and suffering through two wars: first, the Nazi invasion and occupation, then the horrific Greek civil war.

To be considered eligible for an American visa under this new program, a person needed to provide proof of having been afflicted by a civil war and have a sponsor in America. I was fortunate to qualify for both requirements in 1950 when the program was offered, but I was unfortunate because the program closed before I could get my visa.

After waiting five agonizing years, I got a second chance to try again. I submitted my application, and all the required documents, and I was waiting to hear from the immigration office to go to Athens and get that illusive document—my visa.

I was one of many people that was waiting for the mailman every evening. Some others were waiting to hear from the immigration office, but most of them were waiting for their pension checks or checks from relatives in America.

One particular evening, we all saw Foti, the mailman, walking slowly toward our group with a smile on his face, carrying a heavy mailbag slung over his right shoulder, looking for people he had mail for.

When he was a few feet away from us, I noticed a small smirk on his face when he looked at me, indicating that he had something special for me. He moved closer to our group and came directly towards me; his smile was now visibly evident. When he got in front of me, he stopped and pulled a larger-than-normal sized envelope from his bulging heavy leather bag and handed it to me with a full smile on his face, and said,

"Giorgo, I think this is what you have been waiting for—for a long time."

With a happy smile and a pounding heart, I took the envelope and quickly glanced at it. It was addressed to me from the US Embassy in Athens. I quickly opened it, and there was my final chance to go to America.

Clutching the letter in my right hand, I jumped up with my arms toward the sky and let out a loud scream: "I am going to America!" Everyone in the *platia,* and those who were close enough to hear me started clapping and yelling, "Good luck, Giorgo!" "And don't forget us!"

I felt like I was already boarding my plane to America, but I knew very well what they were really saying: "We wish we could come with you." It was the dream of almost every person in my village, as well as many people around the world, to long for the chance for a better life after many years of wars.

I ran back home to tell this great news to my family. When I arrived home, holding this important envelope with a big smile, my mother knew right away that it was great news. She started crying with happiness after I told her it was from the immigration office to appear for processing my documents to get my visa.

She hugged me tight and said, "Giorgo, it is my life-long dream to see you go close to my dear brother and live a good life away from all this misery."

I went through the same procedure of taking the bus to Athens, but this time I didn't pay any attention to the sites. I just wanted to get there and hoped this time, I wouldn't be disappointed and return to the village without that long-awaited for visa in my pocket—fortunately, I returned to the village a week later with that beautiful visa held tightly in my hand.

There were a few chores to do before my departure; one of them was the grape harvesting time, one of my favorite annual projects, and as always, before we harvested the grapes and turned them into *mousto* to pour into large wooden barrels, the barrels had to be scraped and thoroughly washed and cleaned inside. I learned to do this when I was five. But now I was 18, and I wasn't sure if I could still fit through the rectangular opening on top of the barrel, but I wanted to do it one last time. After a lot of wiggling and squeezing, I got through the opening, and someone handed me the scraper. I began scraping and worked for a couple of hours, then I had to stick my head up for air for a minute or two and went back in and continued working to finish the job for this barrel with one more to go. All my friends and neighbors were yelling at me to get out and have someone else finish the scraping, but I wanted to do it as my last job for my family. When I finished scraping the second barrel, they helped me to get out through the rectangular opening. Everyone applauded, including my mother, and she gave me a big hug and kiss as she was thrilled to watch me scrape the barrels for the last time.

The next day, with the help of a few neighbors, we started the hard job of harvesting the grapes by carrying them in large woven baskets on our backs and emptying them in the specially built *wourna* (trough) in the *katoi* (basement). It was like an annual festival; everyone was in good spirits, laughing and talking out loud. Maybe it was the sweet grapes that made it so festive. Who knows?

The grape harvest took two days to complete. The next and most important step of the wine-making process was to stomp the grapes and squeeze all the juice out. The ancient way of doing that consisted of a few different groups of stompers to wash their feet, roll up their trousers, climb over the walls of the *wourna*, and jump into the freshly picked grapes, two to three feet deep, and jump up and down, stomping until all the grapes were crushed. Once all the grapes were completely crushed, and the juice (*mousto*) drained into the large bronze *kazani* (cauldron), (where my father performed certain quality tests), the mousto was then poured into clean wooden barrels. He then added wine yeast and pine resin to give it a resin taste that the Greek people like; that's why this kind of wine is called *retsina*.

The last step of the grape stomping is the process of taking the remaining stems and skins to make a high-octane drink called *raki* or *tsipouro*, a very clear liquid that contains 40% alcohol. The scraps were fed to the pigs; nothing was thrown away.

Grape stomping is an ancient method that has now been replaced by machines, although many winemakers still believe in the ancient

277

stomping method. They say it speeds up fermentation and is a gentler process that avoids crushing the seeds, resulting in a smoother flavor.

We usually celebrate the end of the grape harvest, but this year was a special celebration arranged by my mother to celebrate my upcoming departure from this life to a new life in America, and this would be my last time as part of this annual celebration. It was a very memorable and emotional event for me. My mother made her favorite meal, lamb with potatoes, in the big brick oven and invited all the neighbors and relatives to celebrate this special grape harvest with us and say goodbye to her much-loved son.

The celebration went on till early morning, with everyone singing and dancing and a few crying with happiness that I was the lucky one to leave this life. I hugged and kissed everyone and promised I would never forget.

The next thing I wanted to do before my departure was to go to the *xorafia* farms with my buddy Truman and say goodbye to the place where the two of us had spent the last ten years of my young life, working in despair, hunger, and hopelessness.

I went and stood in front of our shed, where many fearful moments took place throughout the years, especially the days of the locust swarms that devastated our crops.

For the last time, I rode my friend Truman while he fed on some nice fresh green cabbage as a special treat.

That day, there were two strong emotions in my heart: one of sadness for abandoning 18 years of my life and all the people I grew up with and suffered with through the wars; the other, full of happiness, knowing I was going to a better place to live with and find new friends and relatives, but also far away from the family that had brought me up with love and self-sacrifices.

Last time riding my friend Truman.

In front of the shed

It was time for me to leave this hopeless hard life, but it was the only life I had learned to live, and I was always protected by loving parents.

My mother and I walked to the *platia* to take the village bus to Sparta, one more time and the last time where I could get on the Athens bus. The trip to Sparta was about 25 minutes, and my mother never stopped talking and crying at the same time.

"Never forget me and the rest of our family," she said. "And when you get to America, hug, and kiss the man who made this possible; he has no children of his own," and she made me promise that I would take his name. "So, take the name George Kaperonis so that my father's name will continue."

"I will, Mitera, I promise."

We arrived in Sparta, and our bus dropped us off at the Athens-bound bus, a large vehicle with comfortable seats, much better than our bus from the village. My mother stood in line with me as I waited to board. When my turn came to step up and onto the bus, my mother, with tears covering her face, hugged me hard, kissed me, and said, "God be with you, my boy," and her last three words were, "Don't forget us." Now, I broke down in tears.

I boarded the bus. The driver closed the doors, checked to see that all the passengers were on board, and started slowly rolling on the way to Athens. When I looked back to wave to my mother, she was still waving goodbye to me with a crying face. We both knew this was a one-way trip with no permanent return.

The bus went through the narrow streets of Sparta for the last time to the main road, continued to gain speed, and passed the city limits. I looked back to wave goodbye to Sparta, a city that I loved. I had spent a lot of time there during the last several years: at least one year while I attended high school and my time in the hospital having my appendix removed.

The bus kept going up the winding road to Athens, as it did many times when I was getting my visa. It went through the same route going through all the small and big towns, but this time, it seemed like it took much less time to get to Athens. Maybe it was because I had seen the scenery a few times before, or maybe because my mind had traveled over the ocean and landed in a wonderful place that the ride seemed to be shorter. Or maybe I took a small nap to rest my tired mind from the fast-moving, happy, and sad moments in the country I was raised in and was now leaving behind, as well as the people I loved.

The other and most important reason this trip to Athens was different from past times was because it was a one-way ticket, and I was not planning to come back to live-- only for a visit.

In 1956, I immigrated to America. I worked hard, attended college, and served my new country as a member of the US Air Force. After completing my service, I met Katie, the love of my life, and we got married soon after.

We both worked for a couple of years, then together started an electronics company, and raised two children. Twenty-five years later, we both retired to Florida, and I started writing my first book, *Growing up under the Nazi Boot*.

Epilogue

When I see little children playing around, it makes me believe that childhood is indeed the best and most carefree time in one's life. Of course, every human being deserves to be raised in the best environment. However, for many people, it was and still is a luxury that they can't afford. Unfortunately, I am one of those people who couldn't afford this luxury. Yes, I was raised in a war-torn era.

Growing up during a foreign or civil war is devastating to the mind and soul to the core. These horrible events leave an effect so profound that you may never recover the harshness and sadism inflicted by one human onto another and then another human being. It becomes even more damaging to the child's character, which is then built around hatred and killings between families and neighbors in a civil war.

I grew up during the cruel German invasion followed by a lengthy, disastrous Greek civil war where trust and love between friends, family, and neighbors no longer existed. All you could see was a father sacrificing his child or the entire family for a cause or for self-preservation. Mothers and sisters took up arms to kill their villagers and fellow citizens. How can a young mind recover from such a traumatic experience?

Nearly 80 years later, I am still struggling with such deep-held memories of my childhood.

Thousands, in fact, millions, of children like me grew up during these catastrophic times. Many never made it out alive, while others survived but lived without limbs, hands, or seriously deformed bodies.

They still want to live but cannot forget how they were raised, carrying the scars of the war for the rest of their lives.

Thankfully, I survived those tough times—times when it was better to be dead than alive, and that too, with all my body parts intact. God saved me, although my soul and mind have been permanently damaged and might never recover from haunting memories of those horrific events. I hoped and prayed that my country and the world would never see another brutal, demonic dictator the likes of Hitler. Unfortunately, my hopes and prayers failed me because another Hitler-like dictator, Vladimir Putin, is killing thousands and soon millions of innocent human beings in Ukraine—millions of children are living the same life as I did 75 years ago.

Greek Words with English Meanings

Greek	English
Dexameni	Water tank
Drepani	Sickle
Fourno	Brick oven
Glyka	Greek sweets
Hilopites	Noodles
Horio	Village
Karveli	Loaf
Katoi	Animal house
Kavales	A game name
Laenes	Large ceramic storage vases
Litrivio	Olive processing mill
Mandra	Gate
Mandri	Goat house
Pezoules	Farm lots
Plynterio	Laundry
Sakouli	Sack
Sitari	Wheat
Tapsi	Cooking pan
Taratsa	Terrace
Topi	Ball made from rags
Trahana	Oatmeal like made from wheat

Vrisi	Water faucet
Aletri	Plow
Aloni	Threshing floor
Apothiki	Storage room
Argalio	Manual weaving machine
Avlakia	Water channels
Avli	Courtyard
Barba	Uncle

Bibliographies

The wild and twisted Branch. By Angelo Metropoulos

Blitzed by Norman Ohler. Drugs in the Third Reich

Greece 1947-1967 By Heinz A. Richter

The Greek civil war By YiridonPlakoudass

The Greek civil war. By L Sklavos and VN Gelis

Sources

https://www.greka.com (Agricultural Museum of Mykonos)

https://www.greeka.com/cyclades/mykonos/sightseeing/mykonos-agricultural-museum/

https://www.ancient.eu/

https://www.ww2wrecks.com/

https://www.inewsgr.com/23/paradosiako-alonisma-sto-valtesiniko-gortynias.htm

https://www.warhistoryonline.com/

https://www.enotes.com/homework-help/why-did-the-byzantine-empire-finally-fall-320850

https://www.ancient.eu/article/1041/the-origin-and-history-of-the-bcece-dating-system/

https://www.theguardian.com/media/2015/mar/28/readers-editor-on-athens-44-british-army

https://discovergreece.ru/en/location/western-greece/mesolongi-history/

https://www.smithsonianmag.com/history/the-ambush-that-changed-history-72636736/

https://www.opendemocracy.net/en/can-europe-make-it/look-back-in-prudence-civil-war-legacies-and-crisis-in-greece-today/

https://www.historyhit.com/

https://communistcrimes.org/en/countries/greece

https://www.khanacademy.org/humanities/world-history/medieval-times/byzantine-empire/a/byzantine-culture-and-society

https://www.britannica.com/

https://www.fandom.com/

http://www.occupation-
memories.org/en/project/sammlung/Zeitzeugenkategorien/Zeitzeugen-
von-Massakern/index.html

https://www.ancient.eu/

https://www.history.com/this-day-in-history/mussolini-falls-from-power

https://www.ancient.eu/article/1041/the-origin-and-history-of-the-bcece-
dating-system/

https://www.atlasobscura.com/places/the-well-of-meligalas

https://www.time.com/

Encephalos, 77-81, 2013

Presentation at the Colloquium: "Economic Crisis: Consequences on the
Family and the Moral Values," ATHENS, MARCH 8, 2013

https://www.hellenicnews.com/ (Hellenic News of America)

https://www.nytimes.com/ (NY Times)

Time.com

Author's Request

To my readers

I hope you've enjoyed reading my tumultuous life story, though I may not say that you have enjoyed every bit of it. There are millions of people like me who lost their childhood lives to these devastating wars, and unfortunately, millions more are experiencing the same fate today in Ukraine as I did in Greece.

These mindless wars are being waged in the name of ideologies, caste, religion, and power.

My story is a testament to what happens to millions of people when one dictator exercises his quest for power and wages a brutal, destructive war to achieve it.

Putting my heart on paper was not at all an easy task for me; many a time, writing this book triggered episodes of emotional trauma. However, I gained the strength to continue writing my story in the hopes and desire to stop, if that was ever possible, these devastating wars.

Please, share your thoughts, experiences, and feedback on Amazon or any of the other platforms from where you have purchased my book. I will continue my work and bring you more books based on real-life stories. Your review is extremely important to me and will be much appreciated.

Thank you very much.

Made in the USA
Middletown, DE
22 June 2023

33242982R00166